ON MORAL
GROUNDS

ON MORAL GROUNDS

The Art/Science of Ethics

Daniel C. Maguire
and
A. Nicholas Fargnoli

CROSSROAD • NEW YORK

1991

The Crossroad Publishing Company
370 Lexington Avenue, New York, NY 10017

Printed in the United States of America
Typesetting output: TEXSource, Houston

Library of Congress Cataloging-in-Publication Data

Maguire, Daniel C.
On moral grounds : the art, science of ethics / Daniel C. Maguire
and A. Nicholas Fargnoli.
p. cm.
Includes bibliographical references and index.
ISBN 0-8245-1123-9
1. Ethics. I. Fargnoli, A. Nicholas. II. Title.
BJ1012.M35 1991
170—dc20   91-18224
                                                        CIP

*To all our students
who prove that the morally inquisitive mind
is as much a part of human nature
as is the instinct to breathe.*

Contents

PART FIVE
Avoiding the Hazards of Moral Discourse

Introduction

Our age can lay claim to a unique moral chaos. Modernity badgers us with perplexing moral questions: Can good ethics and good business ever coincide? Should medical science do all the things that it now can do? Is truth-telling always a virtue? If it is, how can one maintain professional or personal confidentiality? Is honesty always the best policy? What are the proper criteria for the journalistic media when it comes to reporting the real news and avoiding sensationalism? Should there be an "ethics committee" in government, in business, in hospitals, in law firms, or in financial centers? How would an ethics committee function in such places?

Though every age thinks its own the worst, our immorality is at least impressive: drug abuse, the careless spread of AIDS, pollution on land, sea, and air. Some business people defend as essential to their competitive positions almost anything that they can get away with. Is profit the only goal of business? Scandals reveal the systemic corruption in parts of political and corporate life. Bribes, wheeling and dealing, influence peddling, and cheating seem, at times, to be ubiquitous. No value seems secure.

Walking or travelling some of our urban streets requires the courage of a roughrider. The United States spends more than nine thousand dollars a second for "defense," and yet we are afraid to walk around the block at night. Even the system of justice and law is not always trusted. Just as a simpler America expected honesty, we expect the opposite. Cynicism about public institutions is rampant.

Our scientific powers throw moral questions at us daily. Science seems to have normalized surprise. Should we do some of the things that we suddenly and terrifyingly can do? What moral standards govern genetic engineering, surrogate mothering, freezing embryos for later implantation, or research on externally growing human embryos? Should we use the tissues from aborted fetuses to heal the sick? Should we keep people alive regardless of the quality of that life? What about our obligations to the environment now that, for the first time in history, we can destroy faster than nature can repair?

Militarily powerful nations have prepared the wherewithal to end the world and stored it in their silos and submarines. As the surrealistic potential for nuclear and biological warfare spreads, the question arises as to how much moral intelligence is operating on this planet. A hole larger than the continent of Australia is found in the ozone layer over

Antarctica. Is the human mind really at work on planet earth or is there a thought-free, unmanageable momentum rushing us to terracide and disaster?

At the same time, moral opportunity beckons even amid the chaos. We now have the technical genius to end hunger and poverty, but do we have the moral wisdom and will? We have the know-how to cleanse the earth, fruitfully utilize its treasury of water and topsoil, defuse the "biological timebomb," and provide the material infrastructure for a peace the likes of which ancient seers and poets dared not imagine. While facing squarely the perils posed by our modern talents, we cannot lose sight of our modernity as a unique moment of moral opportunity and hope.

Where Is Ethics Today?

At the end of the nineteenth century, America lost interest in ethics. To see the truth of this, look at the Amherst College bulletin for 1895. The whole first page is given over to a description of the course on ethics. It is given to seniors, taught by the president of the college, and is clearly intended to be the capstone of the educational process. The educational philosophy behind this — and it was common in nineteenth-century America — was that students were not considered educated if their moral intelligence had not been refined by the study of ethics. Return to the Amherst bulletin just ten years later, in 1905, and you discover that ethics is no longer front page at Amherst or most colleges. It became an elective for sophomores or it disappeared.

What happened? What happened was that we had become infatuated with the new sciences. These sciences were good. They expanded human potential and were full of promise. We thought science, well done, would replace ethics. That was a mistake, a serious one. And since mistakes in ethics are not just unfortunate, but may be lethal, it might turn out to have been a terminal mistake. Early in the nineteenth century, the philosopher Arthur Schopenhauer said that every great mind had blunted its wits on the question of the moral. That stopped being true almost as soon as he said it. Science became our shibboleth. If something was scientific, it was good. If we *can* do it, we *should* do it.

The nonsense of all this is dawning on us as we choke on the effects of "value-free" science, and as we sit in fear of irradiation or incineration by scientific means, and as we jog over ground waters that are filling with poison and menacing our future. Science does not do ethics. It raises questions for ethics. Science is a power, whether used in computers, medicine, business, or research. Science, to be human, must be wed to ethics. A society, *to be safe*, must insist on that wedding. Happily, today there appears to be a renewed interest in ethics, but in order for ethics to make a real difference in all that we do as humans, this interest must be more than a superficial passing phase.

The ancients said: "He who reflects not in his heart is like the beast that perishes." That really is not true. The beasts are better off. Even without reflection, they have instinct that imbues them with the wisdom of survival. We have no such advantage. We will neither survive nor flourish by instinct, but only by the educated activation of our moral evaluative powers. As Nietzsche correctly says, we are "the valuing animal." We are not programmed; we have to think and opt amid competing values. Our most important and fundamental value-thinking is at the level of morals. The systematic study of moral value questions as they arrive in our personal, professional, and political lives is called "ethics."

Ethics studies moral questions, and moral questions and values are more basic than other values because they touch not just on what we do or produce or possess, but on what we *are as persons*. It is admittedly unfortunate if a person is not gifted with wealth, gracefulness, beauty, computer skills, and aesthetic sophistication. But it is a qualitative leap beyond the merely unfortunate if a person is a murderer, a liar, a fraud, or a thief. Here the failure is at the level of moral values, at the level of what a person is and should be *as a person*. Material and functional values are not the same as moral values. Confusion about moral values is drastic, and maybe fatal. The only alternative to this confusion is ethical reflection; such reflection is indispensable. Ethics, then, is an essential part of education.

Ethics and the Professions

Ethics is not an adornment for the professions. The very word "profession" comes from the Latin *fateor*, which means to proclaim. The professional proclaims that he or she has two things to offer to the public: *special skills and a committed sense of morality*. Skill and ethics are the two ingredients of any profession — law enforcement, journalism, physics, the medical and legal professions, politics, teaching. As proof of this point, notice that whenever we use the word "unprofessional," we are always referring to one or the other of these two ingredients. The person who is *unprofessional* either has failed at the level of the expected skill or has offended the high moral norms adopted by that profession. Unprofessional physicians are either those who do not know what they should know about some treatment or procedure, or, those who have financial conflicts of interest, who breach confidentiality, or who offend in some other moral matter. "Unprofessional" always imports a defect in the appropriate skill and/or in ethics.

Therefore, professional education, as well as any higher education, that does not educate its candidates in ethics is stunted — and ultimately unprofessional.

The Purpose of This Study

This book offers a tested ethical method that helps us in becoming more sensitive to the myriad dimensions of moral meaning in our lives. In *The Moral Choice,* published in 1976, a wheel model of ethical method was developed (by Daniel C. Maguire). This present book thoroughly reworks that model in the light of later developments in ethics and in society. Our experience in teaching this method — along with the experience of many other teachers who used and adapted this model of ethics — is incorporated into this new presentation. The method presented here is comprehensive and holistic as well as informative and practical. A method, like that in this book, is not an infallible technique or a simple grid. It is not a foolproof blueprint on how to act morally, so that when finished with it, everyone will agree on everything. What it does offer is a systematic way of identifying and assessing moral questions, a way that brings completeness and sensitivity and nuance to moral intelligence.

This method does not require one set of values to which we must all be committed. However, it does require seriousness about moral matters. It offers critical perspectives needed to arrive at morally defensible conclusions. The method is applicable to everything we as human beings do — individually and collectively — since everything we do has a moral dimension. This book is designed to enhance the learning process. Study questions are included to focus attention on significant points and ideas of each chapter and to engage the reader in a creative dialogue with ethics. The questions are found at the end of each major division of the book. A general bibliography for further research and a glossary of key terms are also included at the end of the book.

PART ONE

The Foundations of Morality

1

The Basis of Moral Choice

No area of deliberate human behavior lacks a moral dimension. That which promotes and enhances the value of persons and our generous host of an earth we call moral, good, decent, fair, or right. That which insults or hurts persons or their sustaining environment we call immoral, wrong, unjust, or even sleazy. Our vocabulary is filled with moral language. We are "the moral animal."

The reason for this abundance of terms is that life is a series of moral choices that we face every day, and we soon learn that some of them are difficult, confusing, and painful. Not only do we learn that there are dilemmas but that there are right and wrong ways of behaving. Moral value questions are everywhere: in politics, sex, business, in the rearing of children, in the way we treat our physical environment, in what we choose to eat and drink, in the advances of technology and science, and in everything else we do as human beings. We are always in need of ethical reflection.

To begin we must look into the fundamental and often the most neglected question in ethics: *What is morality?* What are we talking about when we use moral language? Moral categories like just and unjust, good and bad might simply be mushy, ungrounded, arbitrary terms referring to emotional preferences or tastes. That would mean that all moral decisions are arbitrary, not really referring to anything objective, solid, and real. They might be a matter of custom or whim, not something we can take seriously, insist on, and reason about. That, however, would insult our experience.

We know that "moral" means something. When we use moral terms we are serious and they are serious. There is a real and moral difference between being a fraud or an honest person, a thief or a friend, an Albert Schweitzer or an Adolf Hitler. Ethics is a systematic way of thinking about these differences and trying to figure out on what these differences are based. Clearly, Schweitzer and Hitler do not just differ on tastes. Nor can we say they were just following innocent, differing preferences or customs. We are serious about calling Schweitzer "good" and calling Hitler "bad." Nothing arbitrary there. Those distinctions are real. They are saying something that has a basis in reality. On what, then, are they based? What is morality all about? We can't talk ethics until we answer that because ethics is the study of morality.

The Meaning of Morality...

First, one can explain what morality is by clearing up the key word "moral." The following might seem a little tedious, but stick with it. It is no slight favor to the mind to learn the meaning of basic categories. After all, all our laws are based on our agreed upon conceptions of what is moral. Morality is the foundation of society. It is worth a moment to know what it really means.

"Moral" simply means *what befits or does not befit persons as persons*. The term can also refer to behavior that enhances and respects the value of the good earth. Certain things may seem befitting and valuable from narrower perspectives. To a seeker of wealth, the getting of wealth certainly seems befitting, but *for a person as a person*, not just any kind of acquisition is befitting. We agree that there are some ways that persons ought not get wealth and we bring on "moral" language, such as "thievery" or "fraud," "embezzlement" or "bribery" to describe them. "Moral" language deals with an evaluation of human actions and behavior.

Sometimes you will see the terms "amoral" or "nonmoral." These terms refer to that which does not fall within the moral realm. It can't be judged good or bad, morally speaking. For example, a chemical formula by itself is in the nonmoral (amoral) realm. It will enter into the moral sphere only inasmuch as human conduct is involved. If the chemical mixture is a drug like "crack" and it is being sold in a schoolyard, the moral dimension arises immediately and powerfully. How things affect persons is what morality is all about, and clearly "crack" in a schoolyard affects persons. "Moral," then, can mean the opposite of amoral or the opposite of immoral, but it is always understood in relation to human activity and behavior.

When we get into moral arguments, agreement is a rare achievement. That is not surprising since we are debating what befits or does not befit persons in all their extraordinary preciousness and complexity. Thus, international peace groups demonstrating against nuclear armaments and war, civil rights leaders protesting against discriminating economic and social systems, Garrett Hardin recommending the neglect of starving peoples for population control, or white supremacists defending segregation and apartheid are all involved in ethics. They are pronouncing on what befits persons as persons in their judgments, and so they are involved in moral discourse. We may agree with them or we may argue that their positions are morally indefensible. However, we need not be unclear on what it is they are about. They are discussing or at least assuming in a controlling way what befits persons as persons and, because they are making decisions concerning moral meaning, they are engaged in the work of ethics.

Another way of putting it is this: "moral" means *human* in the *ought* or *normative sense*. The word "human" can be used normatively (what humanity ought to be) or descriptively (what it is observed to be). Thus, you can say descriptively that *it is human to lie* (meaning that people do lie) and you can say normatively that *it is not human to lie* (meaning that people should not). It is in this latter, normative sense that we use "human" as the synonym of "moral." When we say that rape is immoral, we are saying that it is inhuman activity; it is not what humans ought to do. Some cultures will show moral disapproval of certain activity by saying: "You're acting like a dog." What they are saying is that this is not what humans ought to do; it is immoral. (Whether the poor dog would act like that is not the point.)

Why Bother?...

Why must we be concerned about what befits persons *qua* persons? Is it because of convention or enlightened self-interest, or because of the command of society or a God? Why not just take care of me and forget you? Why treat you fairly if I can get what I want and get away with it?

The answer to those questions is quite simple, but that should not put you off. We often ignore the simplest and most basic truths that invite us to the deepest insights. The foundation of all morality is *the experience of the value of persons and their environment.* Every time you use moral language you are expressing your experience of the value of persons and/or their environment. If you say that hiding the defects of a used car is wrong, it is because you judge that in this matter persons are *worth* the truth. If you say journalists should be able to keep their sources secret, it is because you think persons are worth the results of that kind of professional confidentiality. If you say hospitals should arrange procedures so that patients can make their own decisions, it is because you think persons are worth that kind of autonomy. In a word: all moral language expresses *the experience of the value of persons and/or their environment.* That is *the foundational moral experience.* That is the answer to "why bother?"

This experience is *the* distinctively human and humanizing reality in our lives and the gateway to personhood. It is the basis of all law and the seed of civilization. It is also the sign of authentic human consciousness. You wouldn't want to marry or do business with anyone who wasn't immersed in *the foundational moral experience.* It would be impossible to imagine someone being utterly untouched by it. Those who are too slightly touched by it, we put in jail. Without an in-depth participation in it, morality would seem a meaningless intrusion on our whim and fancy, and moral language would be nonsense. If human behavior and activities, governments, institutions, and religions do not enhance this humanizing experience, they are negligible and even objectionable, for they are failing at the constitutional level of human existence.

Every discussion of every moral issue, from mercy death to abortion, from ecology to chemical warfare, from nonmarital sex to the rights of citizens — whether we speak of medicine, politics, or business — is an attempt to apply the meaning of this foundational moral experience to concrete and specific cases. Moral debate takes place because persons and their environment are perceived as valuable and because life itself is intrinsically meaningful. Ethics exists as an effort to see what does and does not befit persons in all their activities and to affirm the meaning of moral value. Where moral value is not perceived, or where it is perceived as applying only to certain persons and things, distinctively human living is cut short. The foundational moral experience is not to be presumed or bypassed by any who study the meaning of human personhood. This foundational experience is morally formative, and, in exploring it, we touch not just on what morality is and means but on what a person is and on what the human power of love is.

Morality and love are contiguous notions rooted in the experience of the value of persons and in the lived awareness of the meaningfulness of life. In ethics, we are simultaneously exploring the meaning of morality, love, and personhood. Ethics is not a sidetrack subject. It is central to living and human thought.

The Foundational Moral Experience and "the Sanctity of Life"...

The foundational moral experience of the valuableness of persons and their environment can only be illustrated and not "proven." Like all our deeper experiences, it does not fall within the simpler zone of the provable. What we can do is open ourselves to its impact, see it emerging in certain manifestations of human life, listen to those who speak of it, and show that moral meaning evaporates if the experience is not appreciated for what it is. Finally, we can attempt humbly to describe it and show that we cannot think or speak morally or understand ourselves, justice, or love if this experience is not accepted as foundational. All of ethics is organically linked to the value of persons. We must now look closely at this experience to see that it is foundational.

When we speak of the "sacred" or "the sanctity of life," in reference to persons and their environment, we mean it to be that humanizing perception of value through which a world of moral meaning is born. The notion of sacredness is more basic than the notion of God. Even those who dispense with the idea of God must deal with the moral, that is, with the value or sacredness of persons as persons. Law and civilization are based on some conception of sacredness. Only persons who hold some truths "sacred" can bond together in a viable society. "We hold these truths to be self-evident...." Those who infer that a deity exists will explain sacredness in the light of that belief. It is a functioning category of human existence without which the human animal cannot be understood. It is a notion that points to the positive affirmation of being and existence. Though experienced at times as imperfect, life is meaningful and that which we do as persons ought to confirm the perception of the intrinsic meaningfulness and value of life. Distinctions have always been made between "the sacred" and "the profane," "the holy" and "the secular," "value" and "non-value." If nothing is sacred, or if nothing has value and worth, life becomes absurd and ethical discourse and all law are rendered inane. In other words, if life were meaningless, it could not be sustained.

But how can we give justification or proof to such an ultimate and foundational notion as that of the sanctity of life? We cannot. Normally we refer to a more generic or a more basic concept when we attempt to define something. We cannot do that in speaking of so basic an experience as the value and sanctity of life. What one can do is say that *moral experience cannot be explained nor can we understand our own experience if we do not accept the foundational role of our perception of the value of persons and their environment.* To negate the foundational status of this awareness is to undermine the conditions for moral discourse. Moral judgments are always statements of what people are worth.

The FME and the Supreme Sacrifice...

To illustrate what we mean when we say that the perception of the sacredness of persons is the foundation of ethics, we should look first to its most striking manifestation, namely, the supreme sacrifice. The foundational moral experience (FME) of the value of persons exists in quiet ways throughout the whole of morality. The reason promises are to be kept and debts paid, and the reason we should seek to bring justice and harmony and due process to human affairs, is that persons are valuable. They are worth all these things. If we had not been struck to some degree by the perception of their value, we would find no force in those obligations. If we think of the foundational moral experience as a continuum, these obligations are at the undramatic, day-to-day end of that continuum. They are, of course, utterly basic and foundational. Human society would not endure were these person-related values not to some degree perceived and lived. However, the foundational moral experience is most discernible at the dramatic end of this continuum where its mysterious depths are revealed. The reference is to our natural tendency to esteem certain person-related values so highly that when they are at issue, we may actually die for them. If we do not have the courage or the opportunity to do so, we will admire those who do and will call them heroic. History is filled with such heroes and heroines.

What makes this sentiment so awesome is the one fact we all know: this physical life of ours is the matrix for all the good things we experience. When we become a cadaver, that matrix is gone, although many people believe that it endures in another form and that personal life continues in a new mode. Those who affirm this, however, *believe* it. They do not *know* it with the immediacy and certainty with which they know their lived experience. Thus, believers and nonbelievers in an afterlife are in agreement here: the one thing they know with direct immediacy is that this life in the body is the precondition of all good things. And yet, we live with the anomaly that we are drawn to admire those who risk their lives or who give them up in certain situations, with no guarantee of any sequel or continuation of life and with the distinct possibility that they are giving up existence for nonexistence. No one who does ethics can ignore this outstanding paradox and mystery in human history. We focus on it here because it shows us in the most dramatic and outstanding way the profound depths of that value which grounds all ethics: *the conscious apperception of the valuableness of persons*. The boldest manifestations of any truth reveal more of what that truth is than when it comes to us in subtler ways.

We will give examples of the supreme sacrifice to point out that its extraordinary prominence shows that it is not the yield of one specific culture and that it is not a freakish element in human experience. Obviously, there are individual persons who reject it and cultures where heroic self-sacrifice is not esteemed. Something need not be socially universal to be considered genuinely human. No virtue that we would defend as enhancing our humanity will be found to be universally admired or practiced. For example, the Ik people of Africa, as described by the anthropologist Colin Turnbull, would see self-sacrifice as madness. Ayn Rand, consistent with her apology for selfishness, thought that love is nothing more than a reaction to one's own value discovered in another person; thus, to risk your life for a stranger would be immoral unless it involved minimal risk or inconvenience to yourself. But, according to Rand, it could be moral and rational to risk all to save someone you love dearly for the simply selfish reason that you could not bear to live without this person. In other words, sacrifice is not sacrifice for Rand but just another investment of the ego in itself.

Ayn Rand is a good example of those persons who overreact to the philosophers and theologians who say that all self-love is morally bad. They are, of course, in error, as is she in overreacting to them. Some of the classical systems of morality teach that you should love your neighbor *as* yourself, so that self-love is seen not as a deviation but as the paradigm for neighbor-love. In fact, the legitimacy and inevitability of self-love heighten the point about which we are speaking. Because we must and do love ourselves, we admire and perhaps feel drawn to imitate the supreme sacrifice in certain cases. This fact becomes all the more of a mystery.

Where Morality and Mystery Meet...

The mystery of the supreme sacrifice is a fact that shows up with great persistence in various and unconnected areas throughout the whole of human history. Our philosophical and religious traditions, our folklore as well as our recent history contain abundant examples of heroic self-sacrifice. In the *Symposium*, Plato writes that only those in love are willing to die for the other. Aristotle in his *Nichomachean Ethics* broadens the concept to include the nobility of the good person as a model of one who would die for friends and country. In Christianity, the idea of dying for others as the supremely moral action attains classical expression in the Gospel according to St. John: There is no greater love than to give your life for your friends. The giving of one's life for another or even the risking of one's life is perceived as an act of boundless love and moral courage. In less technologically and medically advanced countries, women give birth often with risk to their own lives, a reality that is easily overlooked by those with greater medical privileges. The act of selfless love affirms the perception of the sacredness of persons and validates the foundation of moral meaning. Paradoxically, the sanctity and value of life are confirmed by the supreme sacrifice.

This remarkable paradox often presents itself to us. During a snowstorm in January of 1982, an airliner crashed into the Potomac River in Washington, D.C. Five injured passengers emerged from the wreckage and held on to the severed tail of the plane. A sixth person was floating several feet away and was the first to be rescued. When the helicopter returned, a lifeline was lowered to a man who passed it on to the person next to him, and each subsequent time he passed it on to someone else. When the helicopter finally returned for this person, who was later identified as Arland Williams, he was gone. His selflessness was heroic and morally enriching. There was something noble in his actions and death. We really do believe persons are worth such sacrifice, even if we personally might not be up to the task at any given moment.

J. Glenn Gray, in his thoughtful and absorbing book *The Warriors*, tells some poignant stories about individuals who risked death in the face of person-related values. In the Netherlands, during World War II, there was a German soldier who disobeyed orders when he refused to shoot hostages. He was a member of a firing squad. What could be anticipated happened. He was immediately found guilty of treason and executed along with the hostages by the other members of his own squad. The incident had become fabled among the Dutch who related it to Gray. But notice that in this story the hostages still died in spite of the soldier's dissent, and the result of his refusal was more death, not less. His action had a certain futility. It was not "efficient" or "cost effective." And yet it remains admirable. If someone whom we had always negatively thought of as ruthless, egoistic, and self-serving did this, we would have to change our estimate of the person's character because what we now see is a manifestation not of meanness or selfishness but of moral integrity. Is it not true to our deepest experience to say that we would hope that in a similar situation we or our friends and children would have the courage not to stand there like the other soldiers and obediently blast lead into the quivering flesh of innocent and desperate hostages? If we were among those hostages and knew that we would die anyhow, would we not still have realized something in this soldier that was beautiful and good, even if not useful to us? If we were a friend of that soldier, would not the incident have confirmed the good qualities that caused us to love him as a friend? Would not his sacrifice seem to represent the fullest expression of his goodness?

Gray tells another story about a German soldier who was ordered on a reprisal raid on a French village. The orders were to burn the village and allow no man, woman, or child to escape alive. He obeyed and joined the others in shooting down the villagers as they ran screaming from their burning homes. When Gray met this soldier, he was fighting with the French Resistance against his own people. Shortly after the slaughter, he had abandoned the German cause, and when he recounted the incident to Gray, his whole being shuddered anew at his offense. Had he refused to shoot the people, he would have been shot. His refusal would not have saved them. It would not have been a "useful" action, though it would have been moral, and supremely so. We can understand his guilt for not having refused, even at the risk of his own life. The paradox is with us and cannot be easily explained away. We are the only animal that knows and understands death and its devastation. And yet, we are the only animal that knows it should prefer death to the violation of certain person-related values, for we are the only animal that has a sense of moral value. The mystery of the supreme sacrifice must not be missed; it shows the depths of the apparently simple but mysterious experience of the value of persons. It is the most remarkable, dramatic manifestation of *the foundational moral experience.*

In approaching the foundational moral experience, we have begun at its enigmatic depths where the supreme sacrifice for persons is felt as noble and not foolhardy. We are not, of course, implying that the supreme sacrifice is an absolute value, admirable under all circumstances. Indeed it could be irresponsible and immoral. In most day-to-day moral situations, the supreme sacrifice simply has no direct relevance, and most of us, fortunately, will never run into a situation in which we would face such a challenge. We make special note of the phenomenon of the supreme sacrifice because it shows how deep the foundational moral experience goes. It shows what that experience can command. Although such sacrificial behavior is exceptional, it is broadly and transculturally revered and admired. All this speaks to the worth of persons and thus to the roots of ethics.

The Sense of Profanation, the Moral Ought, and the FME...

Gray's stories not only contain examples of the supreme sacrifice; they also reveal *the moral sense of profanation*, the disturbing sense of aversion and withdrawal that we experience in the face of that which offends the value of persons and their environment. The foundational moral experience is also manifested in the moral shock and horror that we feel when persons are abused and desecrated.

Less dramatic manifestations of the foundational moral experience are with us in the normal unfolding of human life and consciousness. We can seek to discern it in our more normal appreciation of moral oughts and moral shocks. Sir William David Ross, the British ethicist, said: "To me it seems as self-evident as anything could be, that to make a promise, for instance, is to create a moral claim on us in someone else." He called this a *"prima facie* duty," and he considered among other such duties the obligation to tell the truth, to make reparation for wrongful acts, and to give to each her or his own. Ross said that he could not prove these oughts to anyone who would deny them. All he could do is to try to open the other to authentic moral experience.

Ross seems to go too far in saying that these duties are self-evident, since they might not be evident to everyone at every level of moral development. Life would be more pleasant if indeed they were. These moral duties, however, could be called primal responsibilities that are recognized by mature persons, and yet they make sense only if we see them as manifestations of the FME. Every moral ought derives from the foundational moral awareness of the value of persons. Because persons are so valuable, we owe them fidelity and truth and justice. A moral ought is basically a specified expression of the respect that we have for the value of personhood. Because persons are persons, they may not be bought and sold like cattle, plucked like weeds, set aside and segregated like mere objects without meaning and worth, subject to discrimination of a sexist or racist kind, reduced to exploitable means, misled, sexually harassed, and so forth. Persons have a certain primacy of worth, and to know and respect this worth is to be civilized, moral, and human.

In another way, Socrates in Plato's dialogue *Gorgias* expresses the same moral insight when he says that it is better for a person to suffer injustice than to commit it. The reason can only be traceable to what may be called a mystical perception of the inviolable sanctity of human life. This perception undergirds every moral ought and those who are alien to it are alien to moral consciousness. We are beyond the level of scientific proof here. Ethics, like much of important human reality, does not fall within the empirically validated proofs and measures of scientific verification. Socrates' statement has a validity that scientific method cannot prove or disprove and it shows us how moral shock gives a kind of negative entrée to the experience of the sacredness of persons. Violation often serves to reveal the value of the violated, a moral insight that finds expression as a *Thou shalt not*. It was the question of injustice and tyranny that occasioned Socrates' profound expression of the value of persons.

The sense of profanation evokes a tragic awareness of moral worth. Medical experiments done at Willowbrook on Staten Island in New York can provide a further illustration. In a 1956 study sponsored by the Armed Forces Epidemiologic Board and endorsed by the executive faculty of New York University School of Medicine, live hepatitis virus was administered to a number of the retarded children at Willowbrook. Conditions were a horror and hepatitis was rampant. Richard Restak, M.D., gives us a summation of how the justification for the experiments went:

Most of the children were going to contract hepatitis at some point in their stay at Willowbrook anyway. Many of these would not be diagnosed if the case were mild, even if it resulted in severe liver damage. By deliberately giving the hepatitis virus, an extremely mild form of the infection would be induced, followed by immunity. In the event that hepatitis developed, the children would be under care in a special, well-equipped, optimally staffed unit.

Given that the accepted treatments for hepatitis were not generally in use at Willowbrook, that effective steps to improve conditions were not taken, and that hepatitis cannot always be controlled, even within the best medical context, the exploitation of these children was flagrant. They were treated as means and not ends, as objects and not persons. Important scientific discoveries came from the experiments and were published in prestigious journals such as the *Journal of the American Medical Association* and the *New England Journal of Medicine*. Most people would now admit that what occurred was morally outrageous. Our sense of profanation tells us that the foundational moral experience was suspended, as far as these children were concerned. For that precise reason, the term "immoral" applies. This Willowbrook incident can serve as an argument against *intuitionism*, which proposes that the moral is self-evident, and as an argument for the importance of ethics. The abuse of these children was not self-evidently immoral to many who were thoroughly acquainted with the facts.

2

The Structure of the Foundational Moral Experience

We should now look more deeply into the psychology and nature of the foundational moral experience, into that which gives moral judgments their basis in reality and which gives us the awareness that we call moral. We will clarify its structure and make its nature more apparent.

Affectivity. It is in the heart that morality has its birth. Ethics moves on to confirmatory reason and theory, to demonstrations of the coherence and truthfulness of one's positions; but it is in feeling that the roots of morality are found and nourished. *The foundational moral experience is an affective response to value.* It is not a metaphysical or a religious experience originally. It is not a conclusion to a syllogism, though it may subsequently be supported by syllogisms and reasoning. The value of persons cannot be taught, subjected to proof, reasoned to, or computerized. It can only be affectively appreciated.

There are a lot of practical consequences to this fact of life. Since moral knowledge begins in our affections and emotions, there will never be a discussion of a moral issue that does not have repercussions at the emotional level. We do not address moral issues dispassionately. That is why ethics is such a special and needed enterprise. It calls for bringing your intellect and your feelings and sensibilities and emotions into concert. It also requires that we listen sensitively and attentively to what others are saying and *feeling*. Moral discussions are never merely abstract and detached. There is always an emotional component since we are always speaking about what we are and what we ought to be. Morality is felt and not just coldly intuited.

Again, ethics is not just an exercise in feeling. We have to reason and argue and think with all possible clarity. However, when we say that moral knowledge begins in the affections, that its basis is in the heart-felt response to value, we are saying with John Dewey that feeling is the "animating mold" of moral judgments. It is a good idea to know that as we move into deeply felt differences in moral debate.

The foundational moral experience does not stop short with humanity. It is marked by the discovery that all life, whether it be in leaf, flower, bird, or beast, is awe-inspiring and a kind of miracle of energy and purpose. Our reverence, then, must extend in some way to all forms of life because all forms deserve esteem. Personal life is discovered to be even more marvelous. Here are beings who are the wonder of creation. Not only can they perceive what is and respond to that; they can imagine what could be and bring it about. They can find and create beauty. They can love. They can speak and sing and dance and laugh. They can be merciful and compassionate. They can and sometimes do transcend everything, even their own lives, in the phenomenon of the supreme sacrifice. Anyone with any sensitivity should be impelled to the affirmation that this life is uniquely precious. Words such as "sacred" and "sublime" are needed to voice a sense of awe and appreciation. However, the foundational moral experience that springs from the depths of affectivity means more than our words can convey. We are not just doing mathematics or science when we do ethics, for here we are involved in the utterly serious work of making judgments about what we, our lives, and all forms of life are worth. That is an affective as well as an intellectual endeavor.

In a word, then, morality is birthed in *affectivity*. In saying that, we are not advocating the position of emotivist ethicists who say that moral judgments are nothing more than emotional reactions to particular issues and not statements that could be true or false. Affectivity or feeling initiates an awareness of moral meaning that is part of our knowing experience.

Obviously, two persons who have profound affective experiences of the value of human life could enter into serious intellectual disagreement about what does and does not befit that life. Just listen in on a discussion about whether the United States needs an equal rights amendment, national health insurance, gun control, or a constitutional ban on abortion. In those discussions, you will hear both the passionate affective base of morality and the reasoned arguments expressing what people value in these matters. What is born in the heart is to some degree expressible in the language of the mind, which interprets and gives shape in different ways to the affective awareness of moral value. Ethics, which starts in awe, proceeds to reason. There is no effort here, then, to say that morality and ethics are *just* a matter of emoting. In ethics we think about what we feel and both the thinking and the feeling give us contact with reality.

Intelligent discourse on moral matters is indispensably necessary for humane society although persons may not always agree with one another. The problem of the Persian Emperor Darius I is an example of the perennial human problem concerning moral differences. He found that some of his Indian subjects ate their fathers' corpses while the Greek subjects burned them. The pollution of holy fire was as shocking to the Indians as cannibalism was to the Greeks. And so we Greeks and Indians today, though united in reverence for life, are forever diverging on what does or does not befit that life. Intelligent, sensitive ethical debate is the human response to this divergence. Ethics is not just a matter of emotive preference even though we stress that the origins of moral awareness are in the affections. Ethics seeks after truth by argument, comparison, analysis, and by all the questioning and evaluational modes that we will develop beginning in Part Two.

Faith. The FME is not just a matter of feeling. It also involves a faith perception of moral value. That has to sound strange to most moderns in the Western world. Faith has a bad name in our modernity. To many it denotes unintellectual, superstitious religiosity. It is associated with a kind of naive and pre-scientific mindset. This prejudice is ultimately ungrounded since faith in a true sense makes the intellectual world go around. To be re-enfranchised, faith must be clearly defined.

Faith is a normal and basic way of knowing. Contrary to the common wisdom, seeing is not believing. Believing is *knowing* what you cannot see or prove, but what you still accept and hold with firmness. Belief is a kind of knowledge, although it differs from the empirical certainty of direct and immediate knowledge that we have of our embodied existence. Let us listen to an atheist, Jean-Paul Sartre, to know what we mean by faith as part of moral knowledge. Toward the end of his life, Sartre had an experience that he recounted with much eloquence. At the time he was at the pinnacle of his career — possibly the most widely read philosopher of his age. He met a young couple who had with them their infant child. Sartre took the child in his arms and later described his reaction. He said that he suddenly felt an overwhelming sense of reverence and awe. It struck him that if you took all his life's philosophical work and put it on one side of a balancing scale and put the preciousness he held in his arms on the other, his life's work would weigh almost as nothing compared to the inestimable gift of this child. Sartre couldn't prove that the child was worth all that, but he knew *believingly* that his awe was not misplaced. Belief or faith may take religious forms, but before it does that it takes a moral form. It is part of what moral knowledge is. Without affective belief in the worth of life, moral ground would dissipate.

The truths that we hold in the Declaration of Independence and the Constitution of the United States cannot be proved like mathematical formulas. We *believe* them and many will even die for them. The signers of the Declaration proclaimed that it is "self-evident" that all persons are created equal. Would that it were! It is not self-evident. It is a *be-lief*, and, indeed, the foundational belief of this American republic. To Aristotle things were quite different. It was self-evident to him that all persons were not created equal and that women and slaves were inferior. Ironically, many of the framers of the Constitution agreed. What these semi-confused individuals did was to express a *belief*, a *faith* — although limited at that time — in the equality of people and their universal right to "life, liberty, and the pursuit of happiness." They did not understand the full meaning of what they said. But their words went beyond their inchoate perception of the value of all persons; that is why a whole history of constitutional law has had to spell out slowly just what that founding belief fully implied. Abigail Adams, however, grasped part of that implication immediately. In a letter to her husband John, who was attending the Continental Congress, she wrote:

I long to hear that you have declared an independancy — and by the way in the new Code of Laws which I suppose it will be necessary for you to make I desire you would Remember the Ladies, and be more generous and favourable to them than your ancestors. Do not put such unlimited power into the hands of the Husbands. Remember all Men would be tyrants if they could. If perticuliar care and attention is not paid to the Laidies we are determined to foment a Rebelion, and will not hold ourselves bound by any Laws in which we have no voice, or Representation.

The FME is a process that doesn't happen all at once, as we shall stress in a moment. The words of these revolutionary Americans were grounded in a faith appreciation of what persons are. And that is the way with moral truth. It is a form of natural belief that's deeply held and foundational. Religious persons might go on and explain this faith in religious language, but they are at one with atheists like Sartre in *believing* in the value of persons.

Life is full of faith-knowledge that has its source in affectivity. Every person in love knows this. You cannot explain or justify with reasons the insights of your heart, and yet you calmly believe that these make consummate sense. Faith-knowledge is also a way of trusting that is grounded in the affective awareness of truth. You are surer of your love than many things you see or can prove. How could anyone see or prove that love makes sense? It can only be taken on faith. Proving that persons are worth loving is as futile as trying to prove that life is worth living, for both are conclusions of belief or faith. We know these things and they are indeed among the things most worth knowing. Proving further that persons are worth dying for, or worth becoming less selfish for, is impossible, and yet we *know* it because faith is a way of knowing without proof. You cannot prove that persons are worth moral concern. What you can say to justify your faith is that life would make no sense without it. Faith makes a solid claim to truth partly because its opposite seems absurd and unlivable.

In a sense, our affections are a divining power that goes further into reality than our reasoning minds can take us. Not only by the mind, to paraphrase Blaise Pascal, can we know truth, but also by the heart, for the heart has reasons that the mind cannot comprehend. Feeling is a way of knowing. We often feel and sense more than we can see or explain. Knowledge is basically sensitive awareness and in affectivity we become aware of many things that escape the cold light of unfeeling intellectuality. Faith is a species of this kind of knowing, and no one, including secular moderns, need be ashamed of it. It is simply intelligent to know this dimension of our minds. Love itself, and more specifically benevolent or unconditional love, is essential to human fulfillment. It is not calculating and based on advantage or hope of gain. Love and morality are works of faith, and never has there been genuine love that was not an adventure in faith. It can be rightly said that love is the consummation of morality and the beginning of ethics.

Faith is an interpretative, affective, knowing act. It is not knowledge of the sort that basks in self-evidence. What we accept on faith might even seem absurd. However, it may appear even more absurd not to believe. We cannot scientifically prove that persons are sacred in their worth. The foundational moral experience of the value of persons opens us to that belief. Thus, morality is born, and survives, and we build legal systems and nations upon it. The experience of the moral that we are presenting here admits the incapacity of reason in constituting the foundations of morality but not the impossibility of true knowledge or faith-knowledge.

Process. The foundational moral experience is a matter of more or less. Every human being is touched by it to some degree, and being touched by it starts a process that admits of moral growth that is, at times, tender and slow — and that can also decline. Process means that the foundational moral experience is not something handed down from one generation to the next like a genetic trait but that it must be appreciated and renewed again and again by each one of us. Persons and whole societies both can grow or wane in it. As we grow in it, we become more human and civilized.

Moral experience often spreads slowly, starting with those closest to us. Historically it would seem that moral awareness has been limited by egoistic concerns and by what we might call "moral tribalism" (a collective egoism). In an essay entitled "The Problem of Universal Values," anthropologist Ralph Linton writes: "At the primitive level the individual's tribe represents for him the limits of humanity and the same individual who will exert himself to any lengths in behalf of a fellow tribesman may regard the non-tribesman as fair game to be exploited

by any possible means, or even as a legitimate source of meat.... "
Economically, it might be said that non-tribesmembers are still being
eaten. Our cannibalism is indirect now, operating through such things
as "the terms of trade" and the widening structured gaps between rich
and poor. The value of persons and their environment has historically
meant the value of only *some* persons and *some* places. Racism, indus-
trial pollution, anti-Semitism, slavery, nuclear waste, organized crime,
the subjugation of women, terrorism, chauvinistic nationalism (a form
of modern tribalism), apartheid, illegal trafficking in drugs, disregard
of worker safety and of eco-systems, and the like, all witness to the
primitive state of the moral process. The fact that we can live in our
own comfort in a world where over forty thousand poor children die
daily from malnutrition and lack of medicine signals that our FME is
not at a high level of processual development.

The signs of limited moral sensitivity are also visible in our response
to physical nature. Not much has changed since the time of Jeremiah
the prophet. Although the reasons for his lament are different, the
effects are the same: "How long must the country lie parched / and
its green grass wither? / No birds and beasts are left, because its people
are so wicked.... " The foundational moral experience is not limited to
persons but reaches into the material context from which we evolved
and to which we are kith and kin. Like relatives who became rich, we
have trampled on our familial earth-roots with little sign of reverence or
affection. The moral process is only at its beginnings. This is portentous
in that we are more technologically smart than morally wise.

The news is not all bad. The process is not going in full reverse.
We see growth signs in the foundational moral process. We have begun
to notice the need for handicapped persons to make phone calls from
wheel chairs and to go to public rest rooms. However belated, that is
progress. Slowly we are noticing our debts to the environment. Con-
servationists used to be considered idiosyncratic. The first "Earth Day"
was looked on as a kind of "hippy" feast, but the idea was soon institutionalized into the Environmental Protection Agency. The "good old
days" were not so good at all, as we now know. Progressive ideas like
Social Security were resisted first as socialistic but were eventually seen
as a minimal expression of civility. Gradually, the moral light is dawning that not all citizens have access to reasonable health care; plans are
slowly aborning to correct that. Progress in the FME is possible and
ongoing.

The foundational moral experience is rooted in *affectivity* and *faith*,
and is subject to the ebbs and flows of a still young and precarious *process*. The object of this experience is the value of persons and their
environment. This foundational experience includes an awareness of
the value of others (all others) and of the connection between one's

own value and that of others; it is short-circuited if one of these elements is lacking. We cannot just value self or just value others and be integral. We must see their link.

Ultimately, the capacity for love, the ability to appreciate and respond to the value of personal life in all its forms, is the foundation of moral consciousness. The appearance of moral awareness and of the capacity for love in the evolution of the human species was an event more significant for human existence than the first appearances of technology and art, even though these latter events are more easily chronicled and more easily win attention. That we as a human species have always attempted to distinguish between good and evil points to the discovery of the value of human life, of all life. This discovery leads to the concern for what befits it (moral good) and what does not befit it (moral evil). The encounter with moral worth in one's self and in others engenders an affective faith response of reverence and wonder and yields the moral process to react to this life and its terrestrial setting in a fitting way. With this affirmation does consciousness enter the moral realm.

3

Doing Justice to Justice

Strangely, some philosophers and theologians have had a hard time justifying self-love, the loving response to one's own value. For them there must be the complete absence of all motives relating to self-interest. This "purity" of intention is neither realistic nor necessarily moral. For example, moral worth can be ascribed only to behavior that has no "self-interested motives," Schopenhauer argued in his work *The Basis of Morality*. "The absence of all egoistic motives," he believed, "is thus the criterion of an action of moral value." The enemy that he and others fail to target is egoistic self-love that gives the self a hierarchical and inherently hostile prominence above all other values. The recognition of one's own value as a person is not only not at odds with love of others but is the only feasible base for such love. The need to love ourselves and feel ourselves loved is essential to mental health and normal socialization. It is a rule of nature that love engenders love. Only the gift of love and the experience of our own lovability can release us from a cringing self-centeredness and empower us to love.

The personal life that makes your neighbor valuable is a life in which you also share. It is a participated glory. And it is no less valuable for being yours. Out of love you may sacrifice yourself for another person as that person might also for you. Such sacrifice is not caused by low esteem for self; it is a mysterious response to the person-related values that at times merit such an awesome gift.

Because life is sacred does not mean that continued existence is an absolute obligation. Morality also deals with the quality of life and not just with the mere physicality of existence. Life is more than any single moment of its embodiment and sometimes death better serves that *more* than continued living. There is a perplexing and enduring paradox here, but the truth is not served either by negating the authenticity of the supreme sacrifice or by denying the validity of one's own value. The paradox is heightened by the fact that it is from persons who have achieved a high degree of self-actualization and confidence, born of proper self-love, that heroic self-sacrifice could be anticipated. (A morbid self-sacrifice is possible from a number of psychiatric causes. These, however, would not be perceived as heroic when fully understood).

Self-love is legitimate and unavoidable also because of the very nature of moral values, values that shape us as persons. If we are clumsy,
poor at mathematics, nonaffluent, or ugly by common standards, it is
unfortunate. We lack certain values, but it does not make us bad people, because the values we lack are not moral values. Such nonmoral
values do not make us but grace our presence. *Moral values make us
what we are as persons; they make us human.* Failure here is drastic and
not just unfortunate.

To be moral by being benevolent, fair, and just to others is also
good for the self. It is self-serving in the good sense and gives us self-
fulfillment. Even Schopenhauer in his assessment of self-love had to
admit that "conduct having real moral worth...leaves behind a certain
self-satisfaction which is called the approval of conscience." This conclusion is understandable since it is humanly normal (that is, humanly
normative) to be moral and hence it has its own built-in satisfactions.
By the very nature of moral value, being moral is self-love as well as
love of the other. *How* you love yourself in relation to others is where
the ethical questions rise.

Justice as the Minimal Shape of Other-love...

The foundational moral experience includes a positive response to the
value of self and of others and an appreciation of the link between
the two. In order to explain the basic response to the value of others,
we must turn to the generic concept of justice. Justice is the minimal
manifestation of the foundational moral experience and the minimal
manifestation of other-love.

Justice is the least we can do in response to the value of persons. It
is love in embryonic form. When this justice-love matures, it moves beyond its concerns for rights and obligations and is transformed into the
superior dynamism of love, friendship, and community. Community is
friendship at a societal level. Since love is not in full bloom in society,
justice presents itself as the minimal expression of moral sentiment.
What we are beginning here is the philosophical spelling out of the
implications of the FME. Moral concern is a never-ending process in
which all our faculties conspire to discover, in more specific ways, what
does or does not befit the dignity of persons and their environment.
The whole of the method developed throughout this book discusses
the process and the various ways that are required to argue morally
defensible conclusions. In citing justice as the minimal expression of
morality, we are drawing on many cultural and intellectual resources.
It is not arbitrary to say that justice can be seen to be the only coherent
and fruitful basis for a moral and viable society.

Justice is variously and sometimes narrowly defined. But in its
broadest meaning, justice, as Aristotle says, is "not part of virtue but

virtue entire, nor is the contrary injustice a part of vice but vice entire." Justice is fairness and it means giving others their rightful due as persons. Justice is the first fruit of the foundational moral experience, that is, the fruit of the experience of the value of persons and their environment. It is said of the value or sanctity of life that it is so basic a notion that life is unlivable if it is not allowed. The same can be said of justice because its absence would subject human existence to unbearable chaos. Without some achievement of justice, human society as such disintegrates. All laws are efforts to express justice. A law that is not *just* is no law at all.

It seems true to say with Cicero that people are called good chiefly from their justice or to say with Plutarch that persons are honorable if their relations are just. So what then is justice and why do we see it as the primordial and minimal expression of our perception of the value and dignity of persons?

Basically it can be said that there are three kinds of justice: *individual justice*, *distributive justice*, and *social justice*. All three forms of justice involve rendering to others what their due is, and without all three there is no justice. Justice is the first expression of our response to the value of persons, and it recognizes that their value is such that they may lay claims on us. Justice is the first of many virtues telling us how we should respond to persons in view of what they are. In its relationship to other virtues, justice is not seen as simply the first among equals. Rather, it is the first-line response to the value of life. All of ethics, i.e., judging what befits persons as persons, is based upon some *anthropology*, on some conception of what persons are. One's anthropology or conception of personhood first shines through in the explanation one offers of justice. The definition of the three forms of justice will show this fact to be so. The model on p. 30 illustrates the three forms that justice takes. All three forms of justice are essential. There is no justice unless all three forms are realized to some degree.

Individual justice renders what is due in relationships between individual persons, or between discernibly individual social entities such as nation-states or corporations. (More clumsily, it could be called inter-individual justice, but the term "individual" will do.) Examples are agreements or contracts to mow someone's lawn for a certain price, or a sale by Ford to Chrysler of some automotive parts. Negatively, individual justice would involve reparation for harm done. If I stole your bike, I owe you a bike's worth of reparation. Notice that individual justice is marked by equality and freedom. I needn't bother to deal with you about your lawn and Ford might not decide to trade with Chrysler. There is freedom at this level of justice. Also, if we do deal, it should be on an equal basis. The lawn-cutting and the price should be equal, and so for all contracts. This form of justice is highly de-

Common Good

Generic Demands
respect and hope for all
including the environment

Specific Demands
taxes
jury duty
affirmative action
eminent domain
etc.

Agents of Distributive Justice
government
corporations
lobbies
schools
arts
churches and synagogues
citizens and citizen groups

Marks of Social Justice
equality and liberty
diminished
sacrificial sharing

Social Justice

Distributive Justice

← *Individual Justice* →

Individual   Marks of Individual Justice   *Individual*
equality and liberty

veloped in American culture and we have an army of lawyers waiting to enforce it.

Social justice represents the debts of the individual citizen to the social whole or the common good. Every nation knows that we have debts to the common good. Every nation taxes and drafts citizens to do jury duty or public service when necessary. Notice that social justice does not involve *equality* or *freedom*. Taxes, jury duty, military drafts, and affirmative action programs are not voluntary programs. They don't work on a basis of free choice. Neither are they equal, since not everyone is drafted and not everyone drafted gets the same treatment or assignment. Not everyone pays the same amount or proportion of taxes. The reason is that social justice looks to the *needs* of the common good. And needs are not equal. Meeting *essential needs* is also not optional or free. No government *suggests* that we pay taxes out of the goodness of our hearts. Social justice seeks to meet needs that are too basic to be optional or left to voluntary programs. We don't seek volunteers for our juries.

This causes a great deal of confusion in American culture because we tend to be fixated in our imagination at the level of individual justice, which is characterized by equality and freedom. Neither equality nor liberty reign in social justice and that makes Americans, with their

penchant for extreme individualism, suspicious of programs or policies that meet social needs. Of course, the complete individualist is a
freakish and rare bird, since most people, even American individual-
ists admit of some manifestation of social justice, such as payment of
taxes and fines or admitting the rights of draft and eminent domain.
Extreme forms of communism have similar problems since they are fixated at the social level and downplay individual rights. What is needed
is a creative tension among all forms of justice.

Distributive justice directs the fair distribution of goods and burdens to the citizens by those who hold power and the wealth that
accumulates in any political and economic community. It moves from
the social whole to the individual. The agents of distributive justice
are listed on the right side of the model. The government is the prime
agent of distributive justice. Government can even be defined morally
as the primary agent of the common good. Other agents have debts
to the common good (social justice), but government does not function for profit and growth like corporations, nor does it seek to build
a private nest like a family. Its purpose is the promotion of the "general welfare." All the other agencies listed have distributive power and
must use it justly. Even individual citizens through their voluntary associations can influence political and corporate power, and they have
an obligation in justice to do so.

Justice, therefore, moves between individuals (individual justice),
from individuals to the common good (social justice), and from the
coffers and powers of our common life back to individuals (distributive justice). In each case persons are rendering what is due to others.
We pay what we owe to other individuals (individual); or the society
through its official representatives distributes what is due to individuals (distributive); or we give what is due to society in the form of such
things as taxes, military service, and social action for the common good
(social).

When we allege that there should be an even stress on all three
forms of justice, we are establishing a basic anthropology upon which
a system of ethics will be based. We submit that if there is excessive
emphasis upon the individual or upon the social whole, our view of
what persons are is distorted.

We are individuals, but we are individuals in society; in other words,
we are *socialindividuals*, even if such a word does not exist in our dic-
tionaries. Just persons in this view must not only pay their debts and
make due reparation to those they have wronged or with whom they
have contracted (individual justice), but they must also pay their debts
to the social whole so as to fulfill their human duty to create a society
marked by equity and harmony. We are social beings not by contract or
convenience but by our very nature, and both social and distributive

justice reflect that sociality. Our basic ethical anthropology may not prescind from that fact or limit discussion of our debts to the inter-individual level, as the spirit of individualism would have us do. To do so distorts our nature and constitutes an ethical error of a foundational sort, since it defines persons atomistically and nonsocially. It is similarly inaccurate to so stress our sociality as to downgrade our individuality, as is done in collectivist theories. The balancing tension between the one and the many is real and must be maintained in one's fundamental view of personhood. A stress on all three forms of justice does maintain this balance and does present us with a fundamental view of what personhood entails. A denial of these forms of justice is an invitation to chaos.

Notice here that we have moved a reflective step beyond the foundational moral experience. We said that it involves (1) a respect for one's self, (2) a respect for others, and (3) a recognition of the link between the two. Justice, as explained, gives theoretical formulation to all this and stresses that respect for others unfolds in a social context, not in a context of atomistic, separatist individualism. Justice, of course, is not enough. It is only the minimal expression of what respect for persons entails. In fact, justice should be superseded by friendship as our regard for others matures. "When men are friends," Aristotle writes, "they have no need of justice." Both justice and friendship, as Thomas Aquinas says, are forms of sharing. Friends share at such a generous, unmeasured level that the lesser sharing of justice becomes irrelevant. That is what Aristotle was saying.

Justice is pointed toward friendship; it is incipient friendship. And justice sets the stage upon which friendship in society may grow. It also serves to give us the earliest intimations of the least we should do in response to the value and dignity of persons — the discovery of which is the beginning of ethics.

Every legal system and every government are working out the theory of justice. If you were to look at every one of the some 160 nations in the United Nations, you would see that they are making sure that all three forms of justice are operating with some adequacy. If any of the forms of justice were radically missing, the nation would collapse into confusion. Justice is the bulwark of every society. All governmental and corporate power is under the authority of justice.

Morality is not just a matter of private life. Governments and corporations do not exist in a moral vacuum. The corporations that submitted bids to build Hitler's ovens could not say they were simply doing "business." They were also participating in social and distributive *injustice*. Corporations that knowingly do damage to our environment may be able to do so legally (due to imperfections in the law), but they cannot do so morally.

4

Ethics as the Strategy of Justice and Love

Ethics is a matter of method. There is a difference between moral and immoral, between Francis of Assisi and Attila the Hun, between a sycophant and a prophet, a conniving coward and a heroine, between professional integrity and moral unprofessionalism. How do you tell the difference in hard cases? Spotting the difference between Mother Teresa and some nefarious robber takes no special method of ethics. But knowing how to reconcile confidentiality and the demands of secrecy, judging the reasons for and against a divorce, knowing the difference between treating or overtreating the terminally ill, distinguishing the rights of the pregnant woman from the rights of the fetus — all these require some helping method. When we discuss morality, we are involved in *ought-talk*. We are saying what ought or ought not be in view of what persons deserve. To be effective in this ought-talk we need a method.

It might seem that ethics is simple. If we agree that murdering and thieving and lying are immoral, then let us simply cease and desist from them and persuade or constrain others to do likewise. Why tax the mind with ethical inquiry? But ethics is necessary. There are problems that force themselves on us and make us do ethics. The first problem is that there is not always an obvious difference between what is moral and what is immoral. Moral clarity is seldom simple. There is increasingly less agreement on our moral choices and obligations in a complexifying world. Second, even if we become clear about what our obligations are, those obligations often collide. The obligation to stop the spread of a disease like AIDS and the obligation to respect the confidence of the AIDS patient present a collision that requires ethical discernment.

The more that history and communications spread our horizons regarding past and present ethical views, the more divergence we discover. The range of moral beliefs is enormous, so enormous that there is a theory called "relativism," which essentially states that the moral is defined by social custom. There was surprise some years ago to learn that some Eskimos once viewed marital fidelity differently from us. In their hospitality, Eskimo men might lend both bed and wife to a visitor. Also, their elders would perform suicide to ease food pressures. Some societies look on cheating as a sign of admirable prowess and others have standards of honesty that would make our society look criminal. There are some societies that view extramarital sex as matters involving only the preferences of the persons involved. The fair question arises, therefore, whether we or they are right.

In our society, consensus on morals is evaporating. We can find a businessman explaining to his incredulous children that the money his company pays secretly to foreign officials to do business there is not a bribe. It is rather like a toll or a surcharge one has to pay to gain access to an important market. Everyone does it. And then the sons and daughters try to explain to the parent that the sex they have and the drugs they take do not signify licentiousness and moral decay, but are rather the currently acceptable customs of social exchange. Everyone does it.

However, even when we happily achieve agreement on standards, they clash with one another. We may agree that we should save innocent life when it is within our power to do so, and that we should tell the truth. But what do you do if a person intent on murder asks you where the intended victim is — and you know? If you give the would-be murderer misinformation to save a life, you have failed to tell the truth. If you tell the truth, you have facilitated a murder. Someone who always told the truth no matter what would be a source of embarrassment and could never be trusted. These examples illustrate the problem of ethics. After discovering what we think are real moral values, it is often a delicate task to see how they apply or which of them applies when two or more compete. To be moral is to be *just* and to *love* well. But how to be just and to love well amid conflicting value claims is the problem. Morality needs a method of discernment and that method is called "ethics."

Defining What We Are Doing...

Ethics is often misunderstood to mean almost anything from etiquette to the study of customs, so the first thing we must do is define it. *Ethics is the art/science that seeks to bring sensitivity and method to the discernment of moral values.* It is neither a pure art nor a pure science, but it is the *way* we do our systematic thinking about moral values.

Art. Although its focus is not on aesthetic but on moral values, ethics is like art because it involves the practice and the use of creativity and imagination, sensitivity and taste. Art is something practiced and lived, and so too is ethics. It is a way of thinking and living. Just as sensitivity to beauty cannot be taught in the way a scientific truth can (although a sense of beauty can be learned and honed through experience and education), so also the moral cannot be easily spelled out or always captured in the processes of "reason."

Ethics as an art is not just a work of uninvolved intellectuality but, rather, is, by its nature, immersed in feeling, in a sense of fittingness, of contrast, and even in a sense of the macabre. It involves a sense of correspondence that can be cultivated only in lived experience. We must make clear, however, that a sense of beauty and a sense of morality are not the same. Tolstoy wrote of the rich who wept at the beauty of the symphony but had no pity on their horsemen literally freezing outside in the snow. Some leading Nazis were perceptive art collectors. Still, the moral sense is comparable to the educated esthetic sense.

Since ethics has often been done too rationalistically, the comparison of ethics to art is important and corrective. Ethics is comparable to art. Like art, it is unlimited and, to a significant degree, inexplicable. As there is no way of giving a full account of all that makes art genuine or great, so it is with ethics. Moral insight is like an inexhaustible work of art. No principle, no ethicist can expend or restrict its meaning. At its deepest levels, morality touches mystery. Modesty, therefore, in complex ethical debates is always becoming.

Science. Ethics can also be compared to science, which is a quest for rational understanding. Like science, ethics collects data, weighs, assesses, analyzes, and studies relationships of empirical facts. Moral values are found in the empirical order where persons dwell. Like a scientist bent on hunting, gathering, and analyzing amid that data, the ethicist has an inductive, fact-gathering, and analytical task. The ethicist's goal is to be complete, thorough, and as objective as possible.

Sensitivity. Emphasis on sensitivity is needed to tune us in on all the diverse, morally meaningful circumstances of a case. The moral dimension is easily sidetracked by other preoccupations. When that happens, we often hear that something is "just a political, not a moral matter" or "just an economic or practical matter and not a moral one." There is pernicious mischief afoot here, since the onus of moral responsibility is being effectively avoided. Part of the role of ethics is to reassert the moral dimension of *all* human behavior, whether private or collective, so that the sensitivity of conscience will not anywhere be lost.

Method. Ethics is like breathing in the sense that everyone is already doing it, but it is unlike breathing in that we do not all do ethics the same way. Furthermore, our doing ethics is not blessed with the same instinctive efficiency. We can make a mess of it and this can be serious because ethical errors can be cruel and fatal.

There are at least two general obstacles to effective ethical discernment. One is at the level of personality development and the other comes from a lack of theoretical clarity regarding the nature of ethical inquiry. Sophisticated studies in developmental psychology have shown that we may grow from one way of doing ethics to another. At early stages of development we may antisocially conclude that good is whatever we want it to be. We are likely to be impulse-ridden, opportunistic in evaluating, with little ability to distance ourselves from our own interests or to relate properly to moral authorities. Some people may grow old and die at these early levels. Others go on to develop an ability for more sensitive judgment and can respond to principles and ideals in a way that shows a maturely integrated awareness of the value of self and others. If persons are impeded in personality development, they may "know" about ethics but could not appreciate its full meaning.

The obstacle to ethical discernment that concerns us here is the general lack of clarity about how we should go about judging and discerning moral values. This obstacle is the problem of method. Every person is a valuing animal and is involved willy-nilly in some kind of method for making ethical judgments. It would be quite possible to have an extended interview with anyone, to discuss moral matters and cases, and then to show in broad outline the ethical method this person is using. Probably the individual has never mentally clarified this important aspect of personal existence. Probably, too, the person is tied to a number of opinions that would be altered by critical reflection. But so frequently we just lumber along, thinking and evaluating in ways we have become accustomed to.

Most of us really do not have a reflective method for approaching moral issues. We are programmed into certain set ridges of thought and in the face of moral issues we react predictably. We may have been morally trained but not necessarily morally educated to do ethics well. Some persons will have an unrealistic confidence in authority or tradition, whereas others will rely on an almost vertical intuition into the immediate facts and will lack breadth of vision or any sense of continuity and history. Others will trust firmly in principles and group expectations and be unequipped to handle exceptional cases or unable to trust their own feelings and insights. In all these cases the problem — in practice and in theory — is a limited grasp of ethical evaluation. Many revert to biased ethical approaches and become threatened by those who, through the use of critical reflection, are more sensitive to moral meaning. Moral sensitivity is a product of good ethical method and the proper basis of conscience. Our effort here is to offer a complete and holistic method that tries to integrate various personal and cultural processes of reflective evaluation.

STUDY QUESTIONS

1. Explain how the value or sanctity of life relates to the definition of morality and how it should relate to the way we approach our environment. Define the following terms: "moral," "amoral" ("nonmoral"), and "immoral." How can the terms "human" and "moral" be used synonymously?

2. Discuss the nature of the foundational moral experience. How do the terms "affectivity," "faith," and "process" relate to this experience? Can it recede? How can we say that this experience is basic to all moral knowledge?

3. How is faith a way of knowing moral truth? How are faith and affectivity related? How can self-love enhance the perception of the value of other persons?

4. How does the supreme sacrifice affirm the meaning of the foundational moral experience?

5. How are keeping promises, paying debts, being truthful, and other day-to-day moral responsibilities expressions of the foundational moral experience? Clarify what is meant by a moral *ought.*

6. Show how justice relates to the foundational moral experience and to our individual and collective moral responsibilities. Clarify the three forms of justice. Give examples of each form of justice.

7. Define ethics. Explain each term of the definition. How can ethics be seen as a way of loving well?

8. Why does morality need a method?

PART TWO

The Hub of Moral Reality

5

Routes to Moral Reality

A Model for Ethical Method...

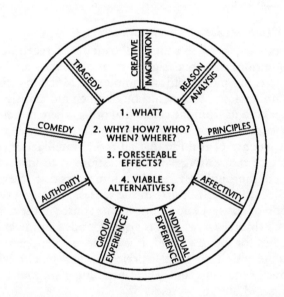

The wheel model represents two phases in ethics: the *questioning* (or hunting and gathering) phase and the *evaluating* phase. In the hub of the wheel is the questioning or expository phase where we assemble the facts and ask the questions that begin to uncover moral reality. The spokes of the model represent the nine evaluational processes and resources available to us personally and socially. Theoretically we ask all the appropriate questions contained in the center of the wheel model so that we leave no stone unturned and really know what we are talking about. Then we bring the nine spokes to bear upon what we have uncovered with our questions.

Evaluation, of course, does not stay in abeyance while we run through the expository questions. As we ask the questions we will be doing some evaluating; the two phases interrelate. Still, the goal of the model is thoroughness, to help us use all our evaluational powers and resources in coming to a moral choice, and to give us a way of establishing and checking out our ethical analysis.

The ethical method presented here gives significant form and consistency to the foundational moral experience and to moral thought and insight. What the wheel model does is call attention to the pluriform possibilities of moral evaluation available to the human mind. This method provides a systematic framework for moral inquiry in private and interpersonal matters as well as in professional, political, and corporate situations. Although there are differences in the way morality is assessed for individuals and for institutions, this model may be accommodated as a methodical framework for moral assessment in both kinds of situations.

The Moral Importance of Circumstances...

The hub, or center, of the method contains a schedule of reality-revealing questions that are designed to uncover the moral situation in all its concrete, unique, empirical complexity. Moral meaning is found not just in principles or theory, although much moral insight is housed there. It speaks to us from the existential order where moral values exist in their actual reality, and where persons and things meet and relate. It is in the experience of real life that all moral intelligence commences. The purpose of the reality-revealing questions is to increase empirical sensitivity and thoroughness. An old axiom states that "there is nothing in the intellect that was not first in the senses," meaning that all intellectualization or abstract knowledge has its source in the data perceived by the senses. Moral knowledge is also grounded in the knowledge of the senses. But for the lazy mind, it is easier to accept generalities than to differentiate within empirical experience where no two things or persons are exactly the same and where meaning-giving relationships are crisscrossing and shifting.

The mind is called to make distinctions when there are real differences, but it can easily shrink from its moral responsibility and prefer false generalization to true and individuated discernment. The following example might clarify this point.

Different groups have been polled on whether they were in favor of homosexual couples adopting children. Approval was uniformly low, running between 6 and 8 percent. Then a story was told about two lesbians who were completing their studies in special education and being trained to teach handicapped children. They considered themselves married and had solemnized their union in a private ceremony with friends. After their studies, they intended to move to another part of the country where it would be legal and feasible for single persons to adopt children. It was their desire to adopt one or two children whose disabilities made them unlikely candidates for adoption and whose lives would probably be lived mostly in institutions. With the strength of their mutual relationship and with the skills they had in special education, these two women felt they could bring more happiness and development to these children than could be found even in a good institution. As far as their homosexual relationship was concerned, they felt it could either be kept from the children permanently or revealed to them if they reached the possibility of mature understanding.

After the groups knew this story, the approval rate jumped as high as 80 percent. This change indicates that when first asked the question, the respondents were probably thinking of homosexuals stereotypically and in a falsely generalized, unindividuated fashion.

A point of method has to be made here, however you might have judged the morality of this case. Because it is possible to think of actions as generally good or bad, the proper answer to the original question should have been: *it depends*, or *generally yes*, or *generally no*. Of course there are valid and indispensable generalizations such as moral principles which are replete with moral experience and wisdom and from which valuable directives can be deduced (see chapter 11 on moral principles), but we must also be careful to avoid making decisions solely on generalizations because they can be illusory. When the groups polled on this question first responded, they didn't know *what* they were talking about because they didn't know the circumstances that made this case what it was. It is fair to say that both killing and using heroin are generally bad. But this limited generalization allows for individuated differences. Using heroin for pain relief for a terminal cancer patient may be quite moral. Likewise killing in self-defense may be morally good.

It is easier to stereotype than to make distinctions when there are real differences. When that happens the inductive, expository process in ethics is short-circuited, resulting in errors in moral judgment. The problem is heightened by the fact that we are born into a moral universe where pat answers to most moral questions are solidly ensconced in our culture. They seem as fixed and eternal as the starry skies above... and as self-evident. But that which is thought to be self-evident usually goes uninvestigated and becomes immune to challenge. Questions go unasked, problems are unsuspected, and growth into the unfolding mystery of humanness is impeded. These are the reasons why the reality-revealing questions in the hub of the wheel-model are really and graphically central. Without a fundamental devotion to questioning, ethics settles for figments or surface impressions and loses contact with moral reality.

The point of ethics we are making is that "human actions are good or bad according to the circumstances," as the philosopher Thomas Aquinas observed long ago. The center of the wheel model represents the inductive phase of ethics in which we search for the relevant circumstances. This phase is often avoided in practice and slighted in theory; also, it must not be confused with ethical relativism or with a flaccid and normless "situation ethics." Because circumstances are always changing or are always different does not mean that there is no solid ground in ethics. What it does mean is that one is always more sensitive to the unique moral reality of every case.

Certain circumstances, of course, might not at times affect the morality of an action. Whether you are robbed on a Tuesday or a Wednesday would probably make no real *moral* difference. Such circumstances may be quite incidental and have little or no effect on the moral status of the behavior in question. But not all circumstances are such. In fact there are circumstances that constitute the moral reality that is being judged. Killing as the only alternative in self-defense is not the same morally as killing while robbing. The circumstances are different and, so too, the morality of the actions. Moral judgment is *circumstantial* in the true sense of the word: *moral judgment always stands within the web of a particular context.* You cannot make a moral judgment if you do not know the circumstances that specify and give an action its moral meaning, any more than a judge could decide a case without hearing its circumstances. The reality-revealing questions in the center of the wheel model do just that: they direct us to the morally relevant circumstances.

The Temptation to Taboo...

Actually, this insight concerning the importance of moral circumstances is the fruit of common sense, and most people recognize it and live and judge accordingly. However, what we might call the taboo mindset is hostile to it. While granting that most things are right or wrong according to their circumstances, the moral tabooist holds that certain actions are wrong regardless of the circumstances. These actions are wrong solely because they are forbidden. This moral mindset can be found in people who have considered as wrong, regardless of the circumstances, such things as gambling, contraceptive intercourse, the use of condoms to help prevent the spread of AIDS, remarriage after divorce, interracial marriage, consumption of alcoholic beverages, conscientious objection to civil authority, and a thousand other things. If they judged that all these things were likely to be bad precisely because of the circumstances that attend them, then we might agree or disagree with their assessment of the circumstances, but we could not fault their ethical method. The error in method arises from proclaiming certain activity wrong with no perceived need to consult the circumstances that undergird and constitute moral meaning.

This tendency to judge preter-circumstantially is especially typical of children. Psychologist Jean Piaget has pointed out that young children do not evaluate intentions and other circumstances in their value judgments. A type of action has a fixed meaning *regardless of the circumstances*, to use the language of taboo. Thus a very young child will not see any moral difference in breaking a cup accidentally or out of spite. The cup got broken and that is all that really counts. As a child matures, or, we might better say, if the child matures, he or she sees the essential difference circumstances make.

Jean-Paul Sartre, with his existentialist's aversion both to false generalization and to the lack of specific awareness, can be instructive here. Sartre has said that the greatest evil of which we are capable is to treat as abstract that which is concrete. If we blur unique persons and situations into ill-fitting, abstract categories, or, if we do not seek the empirical specifics of every case, we fall under his accusation. Moral significance is found in concrete situations and actual persons.

If human nature is conceived of as a blueprint from which every moral conclusion can be deduced or as a normative ideal against which every moral conclusion can be judged (and thus judged uncontextually), then there is the likelihood that a particular notion and understanding of human nature is being used for a number of untested assumptions about what does or does not befit persons. For example, it has been argued that a number of categories of human behavior are absolutely and always wrong (such as war, homosexuality, mercy death, capital punishment, nonmarital sex, medical experimentation on humans and animals, abortion, *in vitro* fertilization, or revealing secrets) because they are incompatible with human nature or, at least, with a particular view and interpretation of human nature. Actually it might be true that all these things are wrong in every imaginable case. However, it would not be because an intuitive insight into human nature revealed their immorality. No abstract idea of "human nature" or anything else dispenses you as a morally responsible human being from the task of searching out and assessing the meaning-giving circumstances of any moral problem. In other words, *no human behavior can be judged uncontextually and outside of its actual relationships*.

It is possible to say that certain things are generally wrong, and when fully described, they may be seen as so negative and neglectful of creative alternatives that no circumstance could be imagined in which they might be justified. A few examples would be terrorism, genocide, rape, and child abuse. However, things cannot be proved wrong by direct intuition into their radical incompatibility with human nature. They can be shown wrong only by examining all the relevant data of a situation, data that include alternatives, foreseeable effects, motives, consequences, and all other morally meaningful circumstances.

The reality-revealing questions, however, are not of the sort that mark scientific procedure. The moral is unique and the approach to it cannot be determined by scientific method alone, as the ethical theories of positivism and naturalism insist.

In his book *Insight: A Study of Human Understanding*, Bernard Lonergan writes:

In the ideal detective story the reader is given all the clues yet fails to spot the criminal. He may advert to each clue as it arises. He needs no further clues to solve the mystery. Yet he can remain in the dark for the simple reason that reaching the solution is not the mere apprehension of any clue, nor the mere memory of all, but a quite distinct activity of organizing intelligence that places the full set of clues in a unique explanatory perspective.

Someone seeking moral understanding is comparable to a detective. This person seeks the "explanatory perspective" that can be found amid the complexities of the case. The reality-revealing questions are geared to make sure that we will have "the full set of clues" without which moral judgment is crippled.

Of its essence, ethics involves us in creative imagination, affective appreciations, faith, insights mediated through tragedy and comedy, and full recognition of the social roots of knowing (as illustrated by the spokes of the wheel model). It is the fully informed, questing and questioning mind that achieves discernment. The goal of ethics is moral insight. The failure of erroneous ethics is incompleteness at the level of empirical inquiry. Morality is based on reality, and if we have not probed the real with zealous questions, our conclusions will be realistic only by accident.

A Note of Caution: Paradox and Moral Modesty...

In stressing the purpose of the hub of the wheel model and the need for energetic questioning in the pursuit of moral truth, we must also stress the real possibility that we may not always arrive at perfect moral clarity and agreement. Those who would study ethics must be modest before they can be wise. Moral problems are often complex and ambiguous. Only those who know their limits can be trusted. Simplicity often eludes us. Thus modesty is especially important in ethics and whoever would think ethically must be sensitive to the notion of paradox.

An uncontrolled passion to get everything squared away is a hazard in ethics. Frequently we are left with perceptions that are both true and contradictory. Our sense of hope and our sense of tragedy might convincingly point in opposite directions, and yet we know that we cannot negate either appreciation. Sometimes we will see opposite conclusions or solutions to moral quandaries as reasonable. Sometimes in medical ethics, for example, solution *A* and its opposite, solution *B*, might both seem reasonable and morally defensible. Aristotle was wise in saying that in moral matters we should look for only as much certitude as is available. It may be hard to rest with such a situation, but sometimes we can do no more. Those who look to ethics for a neat code of do's and don'ts will be disconcerted by moral ambiguity and paradox. The desire to escape from the burden of having to decide when troubled by doubt and confusion is understandable. We must always remember that the challenge of moral responsibility is never lacking in human affairs, a challenge that may not be easy.

The undergirding epistemology (theory of knowledge) in ethics must be humble, since arrogance is a blinding force. It would be arrogant to feel that we can always achieve perfect moral insight. Given the excessive certitudes that many folks have about moral questions, we need to be attentive to the need for moral modesty.

6

The Reality-revealing
Questions

Good ethics is characterized by a zeal for knowing what one is talking about. Asking the right questions is as essential as remembering that unasked questions are the source of most moral mischief. The greatest achievable completeness is the goal of the method used here. "The ethical world," observed the philosopher Ernst Cassirer, "is never given; it is forever in the making." To be mentally alert to moral truth, then, is to be vigilant in observing the ethical world in the making. The questions in the hub of the wheel might appear as simple and obvious but they are of extreme ethical importance. The annals of human moral discourse would indicate that the obvious is easily missed. How do we know moral truth?

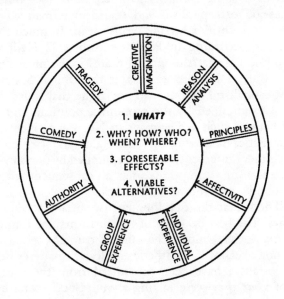

What? and the First Cognitive Contact...
Ethics begins with the question *what?*, a question that is often by-passed or neglected in much moral debate. In asking the question *what?*, our aim is to uncover the facts that lie beneath figments and arbitrarily imposed meanings that we give to things or that we inherit from society.

The word "what" may seem too ungainly, since it could be stretched to include all the other questions in the center of the wheel model. We do not use it that way here, even though it can be seen as a kind of umbrella question that will be filled out as we answer the others. *What* fixes attention on the primary data (physical, psychological, systemic) by which we make our first cognitive contact with a subject or case. All knowledge is a process, but the process does not begin until we have some initial picturing, some characterization or grasp of what it is that we must judge. After attaining our first cognitive contact with moral reality, we have to move on to seek to know this reality in greater depth and breadth, but, at least, if we have been initially successful, we will know *what* we are talking about — we will have a solid first impression — as we set out, and will not be sidetracked from the start.

Moral judgment is about what befits or does not befit the personal situation as it really is. If our judgment of the facts is skewed, the brilliance of subsequent discussion and analysis will be misdirected. The creative ethical mind is always well informed.

Many, if not most, ethical debates result from ignorance of *what* is being discussed. Some examples will help make the point. A good deal of discussion of capitalism and socialism is maimed from the start by failure to identify *what* the terms mean. In much that is said about capitalism, according to Professor Robert L. Heilbroner, the explicit assumption is that the United States is the most typical capitalist nation. But, as Heilbroner asks, is the United States the best realization of capitalism? "Could we not argue that 'pure' capitalism would be best exemplified by the economic, political, and social institutions of nations such as Denmark or Norway or New Zealand?" Other characteristics such as individual rights and free competition without government intervention may be implied by one's understanding of capitalism. Our assumptions affect all subsequent analysis of its political, economic, and moral dimensions.

We now know that the development of socialism takes shape in divergent ways. The best example of socialism may be found in Sweden, not in the Soviet Union. The same is true of capitalism — and the two are not necessarily antithetical. Clearly, many critics of capitalism and socialism have been prejudiced from the start in their assessment of *what* they were talking about. Good moral evaluation (or any evaluation) would not easily follow such an initial misconception. However, not all conclusions would automatically be wrong; but the odds are poor. From false premises, anything can follow: *ex falso sequitur quidlibet*.

On the subject of homosexuality, we find serious definitional problems and well established misconceptions at the level of *what*. What we presume it to be, whether something abnormal and deviant or a legitimate sexual alternative, affects our attitude and behavior. Some cultures are very tolerant of homosexuality and treat it as a harmless variation within the richness of human sexuality. Much of the Western culture to which we are heirs is considerably more negative or even phobic. The *what* of homosexuality demands much more research than many people would like to admit. It always seems easier to accept socially conditioned attitudes (erroneous or not) than to seek the truth, especially when these attitudes enjoy prestigious auspices. A major task of good ethics is to know *what* we are talking about and to probe as much as is possible beyond mere cultural conditioning.

Here is another example of how an initial definition can be controlling. The Fellows of the Drug Abuse Council, according to the *Hastings Center Report*, have expressed concern about the consequences in the criminal justice systems of defining drug addiction as a sickness: "drug addiction is defined as a sickness and through the use of criminal sanctions drug users are channeled involuntarily into treatment where the label 'rehabilitation' masks the danger of controlling behavior." The social danger here is even broader than that realized in the penal system. Chemical dependencies of various sorts represent a broad genus and proceed from a variety of causes. If they are defined at the outset as "sickness" and if all responses to them are seen as "medicine," "cure," or "rehabilitation," then we are starting out in a blur. Facts are distorted from the first. Similarly, there is a broad range of possible responses to the problem meriting very different evaluations. Some involve involuntary behavioral modification of the sort that seems not to distinguish between persons and animals. In ethics, the question *what?* presses us to make distinctions when there are differences and to do so from the beginning. Otherwise, subsequent distinctions may be ineffectual.

The definition of death poses problems at the level of *what*. Medically, the situation has been complicated by the discovery that death is not a moment but a process. Some organs may die while others live, and there are differences between brain death and organ death. At what point in the process do we declare that death has come to a person? Beyond these more mechanical questions of death detection, there are deeper questions about what death is. Is it an anomaly to be resisted and fought at all costs? Or is it something natural, like birth, to be accepted on its own terms? C. G. Jung observed: "We grant goal and purpose to the ascent of life, why not to the descent? The birth of a human being is pregnant with meaning, why not death?" How we characterize the *what* of death will condition our judgments about it.

Another example, *what* one defines war to be is ethically critical. Is it merely another act of statecraft, an extension of politics into armed conflict, and a policy option that stands on equal footing with peaceful alternatives? Or is it really the collapse of human statecraft and reasonableness, a retreat from distinctively human modes of communication and conflict-resolution? How or whether one justifies war will intimately relate to how one has initially defined *what* war is. Here, as in all issues, *what* explores the truthfulness of our presuppositions and helps us to be as objective as possible. Too frequently there are judgments (negative or positive) inherent within our definitions. The question *what?* should give us a perspective on the circumstances and not prejudge them.

The *what?* question points to our power to define reality. We can define reality honestly or we can use our definition as a mask. Defining thousands of civilian deaths in war as "collateral damage" covers over horror and havoc with a term that sounds clinically clean. Our power to define is the beginning of ethical method and moral truth. This is the significance of the *what?* question.

To say that mercy death and abortion are murder is to direct attention away from definition to judgment. Some words such as "murder," specify a set of circumstances (in this case, a negative set). Other words, such as "homicide," give perspective without morally judging. Thus we can speak of "justifiable homicide" but not of "justifiable murder." "Murder" has a built-in moral judgment and that judgment is negative. It says that this kind of killing is wrong. Most people say that abortion to save the life of a woman is morally justifiable. Thus, to say initially that abortion is murder prejudges all cases of abortion and misses the "circumstantiality" of ethics.

G. K. Chesterton said that definitions fight fairly, and that is true. The *what?* question is trying to start us off in a promising direction by defining exactly what it is that we are about. If our initial definition is too general, it will be too vague and mean very little. But if it is too specific and restrictive, it may fail to be objective; it will prejudge the issue and supplant all the other reality-revealing questions by rendering them pointless. If you say that "truth telling" is always morally good, you ignore situations where truth telling would violate a confidence. "Truth telling," unlike the word "murder," is morally neutral. We need to know more of the circumstances to know what moral judgment of it is in order. The *what?* question must never preclude other morally revealing circumstances. This question stands at the beginning, not the end, of the expository phase of ethics. No fixed moral meaning can be established until all the other circumstances have been judged in their relationship to one another.

It should be noted that sometimes the *what* will reveal more that is morally suggestive than at other times. Without checking on *all* circumstances we cannot know whether abortion or hastening the dying process is right or wrong, but certainly both do alert moral consciousness more so than eating or whistling would. Having answered *what* does not mean we know the final moral verdict (unless we have answered it in such a way as to prejudge the case). However morally suggestive the first-stage answers are, the true moral meaning will emerge only when all the questions of the hub are asked and all the circumstances accounted for, as far as that is possible. It is not, of course, completely possible. We will never know exhaustively and comprehensively *what* we are talking about, for the process of human knowing is never terminated in total fulfillment. Modesty, even when we have done our best, is always in order. As we shall see in chapter 11, universally applicable and absolute practical principles are not to be anticipated.

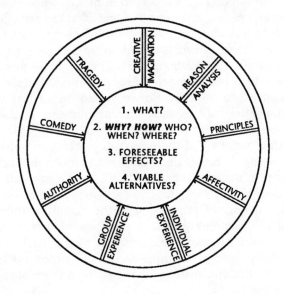

Why? and How? or Ends and Means...

All the questions in this model for doing ethics are diagnostic tools, seeking out moral meaning and morally relevant information. *Why?* and *How?* point to rich areas of moral meaning. Your motive and the manner in which you go about doing something are quite significant in human affairs, as every devotee of detective stories knows. The questions *why?* and *how?* focus upon these important aspects of moral inquiry. The question *why?* concentrates on the *ends* (the motive, the purpose, the goal) that you have in mind and the question *how?* on the *means* that you use to achieve your goal; *how* focuses on the manner, the mode or the way, you go about doing something.

Why and *how* are obviously important to moral inquiry. Two people are rushing into an empty burning house and removing crystal, china, silver, and furniture. One is doing it for personal enrichment, the other to salvage valuables for the absent owner. The *what* is the same for both. The *why* (motive) makes one a friend and the other a thief.

The importance of *how* is equally clear. Supporting one's family by selling cocaine combines a good *why* with a terrible *how*.

As simple and obvious as they may look, *why* and *how* are the gateway to an enormous amount of confusion regarding ends and means. It is a prevalent popular error among nations, institutions, and private persons to believe that if the intention or end is good, the means to that end are thereby good. Anyone who has experienced the harm done by well-intentioned people should wince at this idea. And yet, because motivation is so important, it is easy to think that a good end (motive) permits whatever means you use to achieve it, as the Iran-Contra affair would attest. In that case, people thought they were serving the nation (their *why*, end, motive) but they did so by deceiving Congress and destroying evidence (their *how*, means). The danger in this idea is that lofty ends can be a heady wine. Indeed, all-enticing ends can have a maniacal potential to cover over many sordid means that are deemed necessary along the road to their accomplishment. The widespread, documented stories of torture in a number of nations of the world are all set against a backdrop of unimpeachably noble goals that these nations are pursuing. Whether one's end is "to remain profitable" or "to promote the revolution of the proletariat" or "to make the world safe for democracy" or "to make love" — all laudable ends — the means used and the manner of proceeding in the pursuit of those ends are often unambiguously outrageous. In effect, an end conceived as noble and good can even obscure one's vision of *what* is really being done. If the end is seen also as having a sacred dimension (as is regularly the case in nationalistic matters or with religious groups), it can be completely intoxicating.

The importance of means is emphasized by the Russian philosopher Nicolas Berdyaev in his work *The Destiny of Man*:

Man's moral dignity and freedom are determined not by the purpose to which he subordinates his life but by the source from which his moral life and activity spring. It may actually be said that in a sense "the means" which a man uses are far more important than "the ends" which he pursues, for they express more truly what his spirit is. If a man strives for freedom by means of tyranny, for love by means of hatred, for brotherhood by means of dissension, for truth by means of falsity, his lofty aim is not likely to make our judgment of him more lenient.

Confusing Ends and Means...

Apart from whether the means are more important than the ends, another problem occurs with the tendency to confuse ends and means. That which is a means can readily slip over into the status of an end. A job or a profession should be a means to survival and to personal fulfillment. But it can become the all-consuming end of one's existence, so that family, health, and simple relaxation are completely subordinated — even life itself can be cut short as many premature deaths would seem to indicate. Absorption in the means installs them into a primal position so that you forget your true end. The popular term "workaholic" describes someone who has become addicted to means-made-end.

A similar observation can be made regarding the acquisition of wealth, a quite legitimate means to happiness and well-being. But when wealth becomes an end, persons under its sway will become obsessed with it and forfeit both well-being and happiness. A sure sign of wealth's shift from means to end is the inability to know when enough is enough. Some people die from overworking for wealth and have never taken the time to be happy or to enjoy the wealth they had already accumulated.

There is a fundamental irrationality in transmuting means into ends. When means are absolutized, the originally desired ends are lost along with other human values and are, perhaps, not even missed. The avowed purpose for development and accumulation of armaments is to bring peace and security through the power of deterrence. But there is a fatal flaw in equating arms and safety, and one of drastic global proportions when equating the proliferation of nuclear weapons and security. In his book *The Fate of the Earth*, Jonathan Schell argues insightfully about the incongruity of nuclear deterrence when he says:

If the virtue of the deterrence policy lies in its acceptance of the basic fact of life in the nuclear world — that a holocaust will bring annihilation to both sides, and possibly the extinction of man as well — its defect lies in the strategic construct that it erects on the foundation of that fact. For if we try to guarantee our safety by threatening ourselves with doom, then we have to mean the threat; but if we mean it, then we are actually planning to do, in some circumstance or other, that which we categorically must never do and are supposedly trying to prevent — namely, extinguish ourselves. This is the circularity at the core of the nuclear-deterrence doctrine; we seek to avoid our self-extinction by threatening to perform the act. According to this logic, it is almost as though if we stopped threatening ourselves with extinction, then extinction would occur.

Schell's criticism relates to the confusion regarding ends and means. The only way security will be fully achieved is when there are no longer any human beings. In this case the means literally become the end!

If arms breed fear and thus more conflict and then more arms and more fear, then armaments are means run wild, cut loose from the desired ends. They debilitate the economy and distract from necessary expenditures for other vital programs (including, ironically, those for nuclear waste) and take away from the overall power of a nation. By reaching genocidal proportions, nuclear armaments cannot be rationally used since they would do more harm than good. In effect, the arms race makes its participants (and the citizens of the whole world) less powerful and less secure. The end was security and that is increasingly threatened while the means go roaring on.

By pointing in different directions from one another, ends and means form part of our holistic ethical method and ought not be confused. Yet they are interrelated in such a way that it is virtually impossible to discuss one without reference to the other. "One of the main problems of ethics," Berdyaev notes, "is to overcome the dualism between means and ends, and make the means more and more conformable to ends." However, it may not always be possible to have harmony between our ends and means. We may have to be harsh or, in an extreme situation, violent in defense of justice, integrity, and peace. But such a tragic necessity, like war, must summon us pressingly to create conditions that require less drastic remedies. Normalizing means that are discordant with our ends or treating them as part of the nature of things is morally deviate. The purpose, as Berdyaev stressed, is to make the means compatible with the ends.

In one sense then, *why* is the most obviously important ethical question, but it must not be allowed to overshadow other important aspects of the real moral situation. One must be cautioned against the misconceived and ethically misleading question: Does the end justify the means? An end does not justify a means any more than does a means justify an end. To choose a morally good end does not give one the right to use any means to accomplish that end. Ends and means must be judged in relational tension to one another *and* to all the other essential circumstances. Only after we have completed every question within the wheel model will we have shown all the dimensions that have to be considered in order to know what a particular situation means morally. The ends and means will be but two of the many elements that constitute the moral significance of the case to be judged. To ask if the end justifies the means really makes no more sense than to ask if the end justifies the effects or the alternatives. In moral matters, insight is achieved when we see how *all* the circumstances relate to one another — not just the ends and means.

A good *why* does not assure that all is well. The importance of the *why?* question is seen also when, for example, that which seems to be a gift at the *what* level becomes a bribe when the *why* is answered. That which sounds and looks like love at the *what* level might be seen as exploitation when the *why* is known. At the same time, that which may seem awkward and unpromising at the *what* level may be appreciated as delicately and exquisitely human when the intentions are known. What looks like a mercy death might be a murder when we know *why* it was done. No ethics can be done without an appreciation of the human meaning of motive, the reason or reasons *why* someone acts.

Do We Know Why We Do Anything? ...

Motive is as subtle and complex as it is influential. There is never just one reason *why* we do anything; nor do we fully know all the motivational sources of our actions. Furthermore, the problem of understanding motive is tied in to the problem of understanding freedom, which lies somewhere between complete determinism and exaggerated limitlessness. Psychological freedom is conditioned by many factors: by our perceptions, by our emotions and moods, by our physiological needs and genetic makeup, and by other environmental and social forces that act upon us. There are times when freedom is temporarily reduced to nothing by mental illness, drug abuse, or even by our passions and fears. Apart from certain predispositions or predeterminations, there are contradictory motivational elements in our behavior. Egoistic and instinctive motives can be found operating in tandem with generous and highly idealistic ones. *Why* we act is a pluralistic mystery not entirely penetrable.

For all its mystery and complexity, a healthy psyche has a power for ordering and fusing its intentions into deliberate meaningful action. Dominant motives can operate and give form to our intentionality; thus moral assessment is possible and fitting. A person who steals, or murders, or pushes drugs, or the businessperson engaged in "crime in the suites," may be so controlled by neurotic, unfree factors as to merit psychiatric judgment. Or this person may be discernibly free to the extent that the moral consideration of motives is in order. The working assumption of our society is that persons who are basically mentally healthy have some freedom and some moral responsibility.

Motive refers to an internal psychological reality that has impact on the external world. Sometimes this impact is obvious, sometimes less so. Motive is more than a purely internal matter and more than an efficient, prodding cause that gets actions going. It is a formal cause that gives behavior shape and distinctively human consistency. The effects of human actions are personal and not just physical. Because they take place not among interacting objects but among interrelating persons, they are geared to building or disrupting community. As persons grow and develop in what we have called the foundational moral experience (the source of all morally good motivation), *community* also develops. This developing unity and harmony of human life are sustained by respect, justice, and improving modalities of friendship. Community is something qualitatively better than coexistence. Actions that are only externally good, though less disruptive and not without helpful effect, will not humanize persons into communitarian life. Defects at the foundational level of caring and respect could only be temporarily concealed and only temporarily constructive.

The assessment of motive is not just of introspective importance. *Why* something is done is partially but essentially constitutive of what is done. Motives that may seem the same when we classify them will always be a distinct manifestation of a person's moral process. Behavior infected with sexism, racism, favoritism, or elitism will gradually poison any workplace or professional or social setting. Good managers have to be concerned with moral issues or they will not be effective. In some real sense good morals and good business coincide, as do good medicine and good morals. You can't treat persons immorally and expect efficiency or productivity. Being moral means treating persons with full respect for what they are worth. There is a practical insight here that is missed by many people in authority. It is even missed by parents who discipline their children in a way that insults them. Such discipline produces only short-term gains.

Shifting Motives...

Like the foundational moral experience, motive is processual and not static. The motives that move a young couple in a marriage while they are still under the exuberant spell of early romance will not be the same as the motives that may move them in their cherishing old age. In a true sense, it can be said that no couple stay married for the same reasons they get married. This need not be interpreted cynically. There may be better reasons (motives) for staying married than there were for getting married. Some of the same things done later on in a process may be done from motives that tap deeper and better wellsprings of affection. The external sameness will only be apparent. Process, of course, can also go in reverse. What is begun in fear, as Augustine said, may come to be perfected in love. Or, we could add, what is begun in love might come to be maintained only by fear. Love's lively beginnings might wither or be atrophied in routine. Many of the same things might be done, but the change in motive (and in the relationship) would be substantial.

There Are Motives, and There Are Motives...

Significant moral reality is revealed in responding to the question *why?* Motives are important in determining the moral meaning of behavior and can range in their moral quality from the superficial to the heroic. The question *why?* also directs attention to sincerity in motivation. One who wills the end wills the means necessary to that end. However, good motives can often be the mask of hypocrisy. We all know the popular saying that the road to hell is paved with good intentions. Superficially good motives lack the strength needed for follow-through. Yet they can serve a devious purpose by making us feel that our hearts are in the right place. For example, it is encouraging to hear that people are in favor of racial equality and integration. It is suspicious if they then oppose all the means necessary to that end, such as regulated busing, the use of quota systems where all other avenues to fairness are closed, or reallocation of funds to address the problem vigorously. One who opposes the means necessary to an end opposes the end.

The same applies to the will to have children. If one is not ready for the enormous follow-through, then this desire is unrealistic and merely romantic. Likewise, the avowed desire of business management to be ecologically responsible while not willing to spend the necessary time and money represents a motivational failure. All protestations about one's commitment to good ends are hollow if there is no corresponding commitment to the means necessary to achieve those ends. In Latin, there is a distinction made between *volitio* (volition) and *velleitas* (velleity). Volition comes from *volo*, meaning "I will," and *velleitas*, from *vellem*, meaning "I would like." The difference is one between the active indicative and the hypothetical subjunctive. Many apparent volitions are merely velleities. Volition refers to what you really will; velleity, to what you would will if things were more to your liking. Many apparent volitions, from "I love you" to "our corporation is committed to improving the environment," are but pale velleities underneath fervid exteriors.

The question *how?* is linked to sincerity in motivation not only because it points to the means we use (or fail to use) but also to *style,* which might at first seem nonessential to moral behavior. This bias is due partly to the fact that concern with style is often associated with superficiality. The superficiality comes not from concern with style but from concern with little else, as is seen in those who stress external image and "public relations" to the neglect of substantial performance. The sham of this approach gives style a bad name.

In the terms of our questioning process here, *what* you do may be morally promising. *Why* you are doing it may be heroically noble. But the style may make the action decisively immoral. The Irish story of the man who undertook to inform a woman of her husband's death provides a blunt illustration. "Are you the widow Murphy?" he asked. "No," she replied. "You are now!" he said and departed. It would be hard to criticize *what* he was doing and *why*, but the *how* was an epic of insensitivity. The way people break news (their style) may, like the way they make love, be of the essence. The way people disagree or correct, or the way they reprimand and discipline a young child may make their behavior humanizing or destructive and objectionable. Style is often the heart of diplomacy. A good diplomat is one who knows that being right is not enough, that having military and economic power is not always persuasive, since *how* you communicate and deal often gives the definitive tilt to negotiations. It shows people what value you put on them. This holds also for persons in managerial positions.

The reason for the importance of style is that it bodies forth the inclinations of the heart. A nation that goes about doing good violently will not be perceived as peaceful in its intent whatever its ideological protestations. Help given arrogantly to poor nations will produce adverse reactions, however needed the help may be. Aid that insults will disrupt. The *how* is intimately related to the *why* because *how* you do something tells much of *why* you are doing it. The *how* can strip away the avowed motive and show the real one because *how* reflects the foundational moral experience of our concern for persons and serves as an index of its development. The insensitive may only see *what* you are doing and only hear your expressed motivation, but the sensitive will detect your deepest spirit in the *how* of what you do. The importance of *how* relates to the above-mentioned fact that interaction among persons is not merely physical but rather a community-building or community-disrupting activity. The sensitivity that specifies our style or mode of acting can easily have greater impact on community than what we do. Good leaders know this. Indeed, this insight has manifold applications for physicians, teachers, managers, administrators, and others whose work is built on relationships with people.

Who? The Question of Person...

The question *who?* alerts us to the following ethical realities:

- What is right for one person may be wrong for another.

- What is right for a person now may be wrong for the same person at another time.

- In ethical assessment, some persons are worth more than others.

- No two persons are the same.

- Persons are social by nature, not by choice.

To miss the truth of any of these propositions, something that often happens, is to be liable to ethical confusion. Ethics, which is based

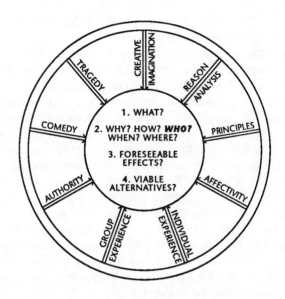

on the foundational moral experience of the value of persons and their environment, must be conceived of as a work of knowing what befits persons as they really are in all their relational, social, and historical uniqueness. A person is not just an element among elements or a circumstance among circumstances. The question *who?* directs us to the centrality of persons.

Like all life, personal life is a process of becoming. A human being is not born with personhood in the way it can be said that one is born with a heart and limbs. These physical elements can grow in size, but in essence they can only be what they are from the beginning. It is not so with persons; they can become more fully what they are. Personal essence is not a static but a dynamic quality expanding life potential. Growth can also be reversed; personal life can become less personal and human than it was. The word "depersonalized" suggests that.

There are two ways in which personhood can essentially grow: *psychologically* and *morally*. Psychological growth refers to the development of those emotional and mental capacities that we associate with persons and not with mere animals. Among other qualities, persons are distinguished by their capacity to sympathize, to endure, to share joy and sorrow, to imagine, to create, to be amused, to laugh, to care, and to love unselfishly. Moral growth presupposes some psychological growth but it refers specifically to the development of human values and character. Moral decisions make us virtuous, or heroic, or just, or they make us exploiters, or liars, or villains, or a little bit of each. *Moral decisions make us what we are as persons.* They flesh out human possibilities and carve the shape of our personhood. Moral growth, then, is the gradual fulfillment of personal essence.

Both psychological and moral growth occur in the context of interaction with others. The *who* cannot be understood apart from its sociality. And since no two social matrices are identical, there is something unique in every culture and in the impact that a culture has on every individual. Thus, it is easy to see the reasons for the propositions that open this section on the question *who?* That which is moral befits and enhances the humanization of persons as they are, and in many significant ways persons are unique and different, especially as their social context and relationships change. What befits one may not be right for another, and what befits a person now may not be good for that same person later. No two persons are the same, nor is any one person the same forever. A doctor who has a hard-nosed policy about "laying it on the line" immediately with all patients who have terminal illnesses will make mistakes. Every *who* will vary and no uniform policy will meet the needs of each patient. No sensitive ethics will bunch disparate persons under one understanding.

Sensitivity to the *who* leads to the conclusion that persons are not of univocal value in ethical assessment. Clearly, such a statement is problematic, having an undemocratic, not to say, immoral ring to it. The statement, however, is based on the fact that persons are not just physical or metaphysical entities but are constituted by their relationships with others. For example, in the pressures of a situation of triage where there is not enough medical aid for all the claimants, some are selected while others are left to die. The very young might be treated before the aged, or a surgeon who could save lives in the crisis might be preferred to someone who lacks that skill. Such is triage. In this case, decisions are being made about who is worth more in a *relational* context.

Similarly, in a case where inadequate medicine cannot save both mother and unborn child in a problem delivery, it may be arguably moral to save the mother by procedures that are fatal to the unborn child. In such a case, a decision is made about which one of the two is more deserving of life. To say that some *who's* are, in ethical assessment, worth more than others is to say that moral worth has been decided through ethical evaluation of all the circumstances and not superimposed from without.

We are not contradicting the basic equality of persons in the sense that all persons are alike in having fundamental human rights. What is meant is that persons are judged in the context of their sociality. In neither the triage nor the childbirth example is there an individualistic competition going on about who tops the other in worth. The assessment is *relational*. Given the relationship of the mother to her other children, she may be judged more deserving of life in this either-or crisis. No human rights can be conceived of outside of reference to other human rights. To do so would be a denial of our intrinsically social nature. The fetus who is sacrificed to save the mother is not morally violated, for it does not come into the world with absolute rights that are unrelated to others. (In the question of early fetuses, there is the unresolvable question of whether you are dealing with a *who*, a person.) The question *who?* addresses significant personal reality and the social-relational value of persons as persons.

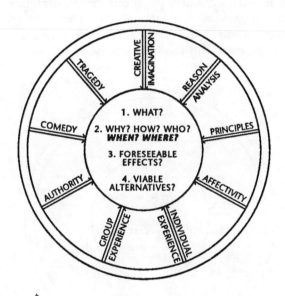

When? and Where? Questions of Time and Place...

These reality-revealing questions may turn up essential and specifying circumstances. Cleaning a shotgun might easily be defensible at the level of *what, why, how,* and *who,* but if it is being done at the back of a crowded bus, the *where* becomes decisive. Making love in public is significant at the level of *where,* given the intimacy and privacy that most people in most cultures associate with sexual exchange. In other cases, however, *where* something occurs may have little or no moral import.

When something is done may be important especially if the timing shows an awareness or unawareness of process. The desire to impose democratic forms on countries that are not prepared for them shows an inability to assess the dimension of time or readiness. Of course, an alleged concern for the proper and due time might represent a refusal to meet the moral demands of a situation. In this sense, justice delayed might be justice denied. For example, some are still saying that the implications of the Constitution of the United States are not yet applicable to African Americans or to women.

Breaking the news to a patient about her condition as terminally ill requires exquisite attention to the *when?* question. How much news should be given and when and how? Here we become aware of the intuitive dimension of ethical judgment. Not all of ethics can be put into tidy rules. The intuitive judgment of the sensitized conscience will be called upon to discern what the person involved may bear and when she may bear it. Ethics can only point out the importance of recognizing that different persons in different circumstances demand "special handling" and "personalized" care. There isn't always a guideline to discover the right *when* and the right *how* or *where*.

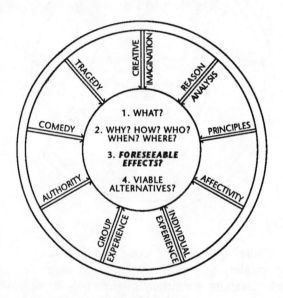

The Link with the Future:
The Question of Foreseeable Effects...

David Ben-Gurion sagely said that there are no experts on the future. Both theory and history confirm his observation. His insight also points to a problem in ethics. The future is unavoidably present in moral action. Our decisions go beyond present time and space. Sometimes the effects of certain decisions are felt for centuries. But in subtle ways all actions reach out beyond the present and enter into the future. When we say that human actions are right or wrong according to the circumstances, we face the fact that some of those circumstances that decide moral behavior are in the future. Morality is based on reality, and the reality of our moral conduct has future implications. Moral responsibility requires that our knowledge follow the impact of our behavior as far as possible. Personal responsibility must extend to the full reality of what we are about. To limit our responsibility to the present is morally unrealistic and ethically incomplete.

Consequences, or foreseeable effects, are of major significance in ethics. In fact, they are so intrinsic to moral meaning that there is an ethical theory called "consequentialism," which makes consequences all important. In this view, actions are right or wrong primarily or exclusively according to the intended consequences. Medical experiments that are done without attention to the informed consent of the subjects might produce valuable medical information, but they are immoral for other reasons. Effects are not enough. The theory of consequentialism is excessive because there are other morally important circumstances to which the reality-revealing questions refer us. One reason the neutral term "foreseeable effects" is preferred here is to avoid any confusion with this inadequate theory of consequentialism that, in effect, shrinks moral reality.

Consequences are a focal point of essential moral meaning. Sometimes this is obvious, as when we irresponsibly allow a very drunk person to drive a car. At other times, it is only by hindsight that we know the morally critical meaning of effects, as was the case with the Challenger tragedy in January of 1986.

When we act (by deliberate commission or omission), we commit our initiative to the future. We may act again and, if fortunate, repair harm or enhance good, but the danger is that when choices become a practice, for an individual or for a society, there arises a momentum that is potentially immune to reflection and evaluation. Choices having become practices can run away with us. Good ethics must allow for a contemplative pause. In one way, the effects of our actions are out of control as soon as we act. We can go after those effects with other actions, but the effects, unlike faulty cars, are not subject to recall. Human action is an amalgam of power and impotence. There is the power to touch and shape the future through the consequences of our acts and, simultaneously, the impotence to control those consequences. Hence the centrality of concern for consequences in ethics.

Our sense of the future is undergoing a qualitative change in modern times. In the past, as Professor Hans Jonas writes, "The good and evil about which action had to care lay close to the act, either in the praxis itself or in its immediate reach, and were not a matter for remote planning. ... The long run of consequences beyond was left to chance, fate or providence. Ethics accordingly was of the here and now." Jonas notes that the maxims that came to us from the ethical systems of the past involved others who were "sharers of a common present." Thus: "Love thy neighbor as thyself"; "Do unto others as you would wish them to do unto you"; "Treat others as ends, never as means." In all these, the ethical universe is composed of contemporaries and the horizon of the future is constricted. Now, with nature no longer immune in its immensity as it was previously, our technology can destroy the ingredients for future life. Suddenly, posterity is the neighbor whom we must love as ourselves if the future is to have a chance. Interhuman responsibility has swollen to planetary size and reaches thousands of years into the future. Never before has the present tense had the ability to preclude the future, and never before, therefore, has moral responsibility for consequences been of such proportions. Never before have not-yet-existing persons and their environment featured so prominently in our ethics. Because the future is an extension of our natural sociality, we must be heedful of ethical concern for effects.

The Problem of Unwanted Effects...

The effects of technology touch upon the physical possibilities of life, and they can often change our attitudes and the way we value ourselves and others. For example, the process of genetic purification must go on, but it will go on humanly only if we are morally sensitive to the effects it will have on our sense of acceptable normality. In a genetically purer world, how will we feel about those who slip through our clinical dragnet? How will we cope with imperfections for which science has no cure? How much wiser will we be in coping with tragedy and inevitable limits, and especially with the ultimate limit of death? With moral sensitivity, science must go forward into the expanding range of effects. And, at times, again with sensitivity to foreseeable effects, science and technology must hold back, brake their momentum, and accept a reflective moratorium. A can-do-must-do mentality, for all its prestige and power, must be seen as what it really is: mindless. We are more responsible for more effects, and for more lasting effects, than we used to be. This new moral fact of life must be faced openly and ethically.

The effects that flow from our activity may be many, varied, and not all desirable. Some, in fact, may be positively disturbing and undesired. Thus ethics must also address the problem of unwanted effects. The decision to remove a cancerous uterus early in a planned and desired pregnancy is an example of wanted and unwanted effects stemming from the same action. The decision to give a strong painkiller to a patient is another example of mixed effects presenting a moral dilemma. The physician might know that the painkiller will shorten life as it eases pain. A business that is planning some new system of automation looks ahead to the good effects of improved productivity and better competitive standing, but also faces the undesirable effect of laying off a large number of faithful, long-term workers.

The question that arises is whether we have moral responsibility for the negative or bad effects of our actions. The answer, of course, relates to foreseeable effects that are part of our moral responsibility. Human actions are good or bad according to the circumstances, and effects (both wanted and unwanted, long-term and short-term) are among those circumstances. They have to be weighed in relation to all the other circumstances. It might be necessary for the factory to automate in order to stay competitive, but moral imagination must function and provide new opportunities, in cooperation with the government, for the displaced workers. It is not enough to look only at the competition-related effects and dump the workers as though they were waste material. That would be to refuse to treat persons as persons and that is the essence of all immorality and injustice.

Effects and the Principle of Proportionality...

Something further is illustrated here about the nature of ethics. Ethics must weigh and balance. Because human behavior finds itself amid values and disvalues, the morally good choice is the one that is the most humanly valuable. The reality-revealing question concerning foreseeable effects makes us face the delicate challenge of balancing goods and bads. When the bads are considerable, we have to judge whether the goods are proportionately greater. If the good effects are proportionately greater, they may outweigh the unavoidably unwanted elements entailed in our behavior. Operating here is the *principle of proportionality*. In one sense, it may be said to be the master principle in ethics because ethics is always weighing and balancing values and disvalues to come to the most morally valuable choice in a complex world. There are always likely to be disvalues in the foreseeable effects of human choices and a judgment that value proportionately outweighs disvalue is not uncommon in a moral decision.

Again, a high number of good effects does not justify *any* kind of causal action. Insensitively pressuring workers to get more productivity may have the desired short-term effects, but it is still immoral and likely to be counterproductive in the long run. Treating persons immorally is ultimately not only wrong, but inefficient.

There must always be the proportionate weighing of values and disvalues in moral discourse. The whole of ethical method must be involved. All the essential circumstances, not just the effects, are to be weighed and balanced in a comparative judgment. The alternatives (which we discuss next) are important especially when considerable disvalue is involved and when serious disharmony seems to exist between short- and long-term effects.

An Example...

An affirmative action quota system, used to establish a balance in society, is a case where a comparative judgment must be made between value and disvalue, and between long- and short-term effects. When a medical school is required by law to admit a certain percentage of women and minorities, specific desirable effects are envisioned. An ingrained and unjust pattern of white male monopoly is being corrected. But there is a marked *disvalue* involved and some short-term inequality. As a result of the quota system, some nonminorities who would have gotten into that school will not. A quota system modifies admission practices. Temporary preferential advantages are used to correct social injustices that have been perpetuated over the years and to create long-term effects that introduce greater moral sensitivity.

The essential moral question here is the following: Is the overall good done by this quota system proportionate to the harm it does to some individuals? The whole ethical method needs to be included when answering that question, and we must remember that it is not just a matter of weighing the immediate good and harmful effects. As a brief illustration and not an exhaustive study, we would begin the argument this way: At the foundational level of ethics it could be pointed out that we are social beings by nature, not by convenience or contract. The foundational moral experience of (1) the value of self, (2) the value of all others, and (3) the connection between 1 and 2 sets the stage for such a discussion.

Justice fills out the minimal implications of the foundational moral experience. We are not atomistically segregated individuals who only owe interpersonal debts (individual justice). We also owe debts to the social whole (social justice) and may have to sacrifice equality temporarily to bring social fairness. We are constitutionally, not optionally, committed to the common good. That commitment may have to be expressed in the sacrifice of one's life, as in the case of collective self-defense, or in the surrender of one's property in eminent domain, or in the surrender of some job or admission opportunities through affirmative action. Social justice may require temporary decisions that are not to the benefit of all. If there can be such a thing as a just war, many would judge it fair though unequal to draft some and not others to fight and die in it.

As to circumstantial analysis of a quota system, one would have to understand first *what* discrimination is in the United States. All the other reality-revealing questions and evaluative processes would point up aspects of the case. Special attention would be due to the foreseeable effects of allowing things to go on without change, leaving the entrenched white male monopolies in place. Also, the alternatives would be enormously important. Whenever there are undesirable effects such as temporary corrective inequality, moral imagination must strain to find alternatives so inequalities can be minimized. An increase in the number of students attending medical schools along with the quota system would expand opportunity generally. Temporary corrective inequality may be justified not because the one can be sacrificed for the many, utilitarian-style, but because social persons may, *in the absence of alternatives*, have to yield some of their goods to maintain basic fairness in human society. If white males do not have a monopoly of talent, then a white male monopoly stifles a society. Alternatives should always be pursued to make any inequality unnecessary. But in the interim of a verified absence of alternatives, short-term unwanted effects can be morally tolerable. There can be proportionate reason to impose temporary inequality to achieve balance and to promote the common good.

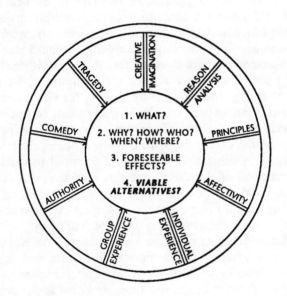

What Are the Viable Alternatives?...

In situations where many alternatives are open to us, it is a mournful fact that our tendency is to see but a few of them and then feel that these few circumscribe reality. Accordingly our moral decision will be based on that segment of reality that our semi-atrophied imaginations allow us to envision. Sloth seems to be at home in most of us, impeding the imaginative powers from discovering moral alternatives. It is to this problem that the last of the reality-revealing questions is addressed. If we do not alert ourselves to the question of alternatives, many realistic possibilities will be missed, to our resultant moral detriment.

A rule-of-thumb estimate would be that in a situation where there are fifty existent viable alternatives, we normally perceive only about six of them. Good ethics should press us to realize alternatives and the possibilities open to us.

Not until recently, for instance, has there been any serious commercial interest in alternative energy sources. The sun and wind are nonpolluting and superabundantly present; yet these sources are not being fully developed as alternatives. Among other significant factors (such as environmental and cost), they pose no threat of nuclear accidents like those that have occurred at Three Mile Island and Chernobyl. Insensitivity to systemic alternatives is a weakness with potentially lethal effects. People rightly complain about the high cost of doctors' fees. Partly this is because doctors begin their careers deep in debt. Few are able to finance their own medical training. Dr. Uwe Reinhart of Princeton University suggests that we make all medical education free. This would not even constitute a comparatively major government expense but it would guarantee that talent, not wealth, would determine who gets into this important field. It would also eliminate one large argument for high doctors' fees. Is this a viable alternative? Why? Why not? However we answer these questions, we are doing ethics the way it ought to be done by looking for viable alternatives.

As a species, we have been creative in many areas. Technological and scientific inventions have certainly grown. Inventions have poured out, and the new world that springs from them requires alternate modes of management. A substantial change has occurred in the social and material conditions of the earth, but this change is not reflected in creative managerial and governmental response. Our moral concerns seem to be lagging far behind our technological inventiveness. Several decades ago, General Omar Bradley, chief of staff of the United States Army, alluded to this fact when he said in Boston on November 10, 1948: "We have grasped the mystery of the atom and rejected the Sermon on the Mount. . . . Ours is a world of nuclear giants and ethical infants. We know more about war than we know about peace, more about killing than we know about living."

There are other areas that show signs of inefficiency and neglected alternatives. Hunger, for example, affects a quarter of the human race, and yet national economies throughout the world are absorbed in developing and deploying kill-power. Swollen military budgets are symbols of despair and imply that security ultimately comes from killing people and not from nourishing them.

Whatever our skills are at the level of inventions, at the level of morals we seem to be lagging behind. The moral world, which involves caring, expressed in justice and love, must always be discovered anew. It involves more than scientific and technological skills. Human skills need to be developed and moral meaning given to our creative inventiveness. As human beings we must discover alternatives to destruction and create the possibilities of caring and loving. If there is a defect at the level of caring it is that we "moderns" are more advanced in handiwork than in the humanizing sentiments of the heart.

Because the human mind has the capacity to perceive the possible, it has the capacity to perceive alternatives. Human knowledge is distinguished by its ability to know not only what is and was but also by what might be. We are not imprisoned in the regimen of the current state of the real. The human mind has creative freedom to bring more and more of the actual out of the possible. It has been waggishly said that whoever has no alternatives has no problem. In some ways, life would be simplified if there were only one choice. But we live in a process of expanding alternatives because we live in a process of change and development. Not only is the world unfolding in its material possibilities, but our consciousness of what it is and what it can be is unfolding with it. Reality is broader for us and steadily broadening, leaving us less and less restricted. It has become normal to see the undoable done, and the impact is felt in morality, art, philosophy, religion, in the social sciences, and wherever else human reflection transpires. Little is deemed beyond challenge. In this sense the atmosphere is favorable to the discovery of alternatives at every level of existence and thought.

Since morality is based on reality, ignoring realistic alternatives makes for deficient ethics. In fact, ignoring alternatives can be detrimental to any kind of analysis. Preoccupation with our creative potential is a characteristic of good ethics. Only a cultivated habit of creativity intent upon the discovery of alternatives can drive sloth and inertia from their tenured positions in the imagination.

Some examples can illustrate the result of sensitivity to alternatives. The initial success of the civil rights movement owes much to Dr. Martin Luther King, Jr., who continually insisted on the use of nonviolent direct action in overcoming segregation and racism. His was not only a politically realistic alternative to the violent means that others frequently suggested but also a moral one. This alternative stems from the perception of the value of *all* people. Another example of sensitivity to alternatives that enhance human dignity and purpose can be found in sheltered housing programs for retarded adults. With some assistance, these adults are capable of functioning meaningfully and with some independence in society in ways that institutionalized living could never permit, and so they have a chance to reach their full potential as human beings. It is also less costly to society. Cost is also a fact to be considered in moral evaluation.

In bypassing moral alternatives, the state of the question is actually defined, or, better, artificially defined. We do not deal then with what is but with what we have decided to deal with. Within this artificially defined state of the question, brilliant minds can operate, but they operate in self-inflicted darkness. The felt gain here is obvious. Returning to the adage: When you have no alternatives, you have no problem. The mind, as rascal, can easily blind itself to alternatives in order to have "no problem."

There is another element about alternative-shy thinking. It is related to insensitivity to effects. Effects and alternatives relate in two principal ways. First, sensitivity to the broad scale of foreseeable effects and sensitivity to alternatives are both horizon experiences. They stretch our vision toward a fuller understanding of the reality in question and represent depth and breadth perception. They also run counter to the desire of the mind to make quick decisions. The mind's natural hunger to make sense of things makes us susceptible to premature judgment. We are easy prey to the facile answer and to immediacy, the thinking that bars the door to the possibilities and broader ramifications of the situation. With the mind's craving for "quick fix" knowledge, we can become prisoners of illusory, short-lived satisfactions. Good ethical analysis works against this indigenous weakness by stressing long- as well as short-term effects and by urging us to pry open our angle of vision so as to be aware of more of the alternatives actually available to us. The desired result is improved reality-contact and better ethics.

Second, effects and alternatives are dynamically related because a pattern of thinking within the arbitrary limits of short-term effects slackens our need to think of alternatives. Overcome by the apparent ease of short-term thinking, the need for the alternatives that are out there vanishes. Similarly, blindness to alternatives works against the perception of effects. When we become aware of the other viable alternatives, a process of comparison must begin that will inevitably involve a study of foreseeable short- and long-term effects. If we fail to see alternative energy sources, we are less likely to be aware of the effects of the currently dominant forms of energy. If we exclude the possible, the actual takes on a certain inevitability and is thus likely to evade critical judgment. In the knowing act, foreseeable effects and existent alternatives are linked even though effects refer to the future and alternatives refer mainly to the possibilities of the present.

7

Ethics in Dialogue

From Value Vacuum to Value Source...

The relation between alternatives and effects is illustrative of what can be said of all the elements to which the reality-revealing questions direct us. By the necessity of analysis, we will have to dwell on the various factors of reality separately, but in moral insight and judgment all the factors will intersect and relate, just as all clues come together and link in the conclusion of the detective. Solving the case occurs when the mind can relate all the clues meaningfully. The same is true in ethical judgment.

Moral judgment, however, is not identical with the judging process of the detective. This comparison, like every comparison, falters. In its distinct way, ethics involves affectivity and imagination as well as analytical reasoning. It is a judgment that comes together in meaningful coalescence. The reality-revealing questions point us toward all the empirical data. The ethical judgment expresses the humanizing (moral) or dehumanizing (immoral) implications of how those data relate in value questions. Before going on to the distinctive way in which ethics moves to judgment, represented by the spokes of the wheel model, it should be emphasized that moral value relates to all that we do as human beings. Moral responsibility is coextensive with humanity and must not be evaded by stratagem.

Many disciplines, such as those found in the sciences and the social sciences, greatly affect the matrix of moral meaning and introduce new moral issues, although they would appear to be doing purely neutral research. When human beings are involved, there can be no pretense of moral neutrality. The ethicist can clarify the nature of moral value, delineate the moral dimensions of other disciplines, and offer a method of moral evaluation. Disciplines, of course, have their own distinctive methods but conversation can blend the contributions of each. Ethics, however, is not just one discipline among others. It views the whole of human conscious behavior and is less circumscribable than other disciplines. Yet ethics does not pretend that its art/science is independent of them. To do its work it needs to be in dialogue with everything that relates to human meaning.

In a university, ethics ideally would be done in what could be called a Center for the Study of Moral Values. This center would relate formally to all departments so that moral evaluation would proceed in an interdisciplinary way. Lines of communication with experts in all areas would further the multidisciplinary study of moral values. The ethician would provide the theoretical framework in ethics (method) and would facilitate conversation among the disciplines on moral value questions. Realistically, many formidable vested interests stand against the hopes for any such creative structuring.

From Hub to Spokes...

The hub of the wheel model is the questioning and expository phase where ethics begins to uncover all the empirical complexity and to learn about that which is being judged. We have thus far been gathering information about moral reality and, theoretically, not evaluating it. But, in fact, we have been doing a lot of evaluating as we moved through various cases. In the face of a moral issue, the mind instinctively begins to evaluate. We do not unfold reality with our questions and then, as if by signal, commence evaluation. The wheel model, like any other model, is abstract but it is also functional. It provides a systematic defense against intellectual impatience in value issues. The initial evaluative reaction to a moral situation is usually impulsive, partial, and impatient.

By stressing and stretching all the reality-revealing questions and by interrelating them, we attack myopia and undue reliance on figments and surface impressions. The spokes of the wheel model represent systematic concern for the shape of our evaluative response to the reality our questions have disclosed. If response can easily be partial and biased, ethics seeks to make it more sensitive, objective, and complete. The spokes of the wheel model help us conceptualize the possibilities of our personal and social resources. They focus upon the highly complex ways that we can approach moral truth. By systematically exploring our evaluative capacities, we may be able better to avoid "top-of-the-head" or "top-of-the-culture" responses to moral questions. We must be open to the manifold ways in which moral meaning emerges. Concern for knowing how we know is the beginning of wisdom in any subject.

Notice that this wheel model for doing ethics is geared to produce better reality contact so that sound ethical judgments can be made. The model could also be adapted as a managerial method for realistic and efficient administration. Unasked questions plague all areas of coordinated human activity whether in business, government, medical centers, or the practice of law. This model, therefore, has many applications. Our concern here is to apply it to the production of sound and sensitive moral judgments. But this dimension, too, has practical import to all who work in management, government, or the professions since, as we have said, from a long-term perspective, good ethics is good business, good medicine, good law, and so forth.

STUDY QUESTIONS

1. What are the two phases in ethics represented by the wheel model? List and explain the reality-revealing questions. Why are circumstances morally important? Explain how the wheel model relates to the foundational moral experience.

2. How do paradox and moral modesty tie in to ethical method?

3. Why is the question *what?* so important? The question *what?* should lead us to the awareness that distinctions must be made when there are differences. Explain how misconceptions on the *what* level can adversely affect our assessment of moral circumstances. Give some examples of definitional problems on the *what* level; for example, give morally relevant definitions of mercy death, homicide, murder, socialism, and capitalism. Are there some "socialistic" things in capitalistic systems and some "capitalistic" things in socialist nations?

4. What do the questions *why?* and *how?* focus on? How do they differ? How do they relate to one another? Are means and ends separate entities or interrelated aspects of a moral situation? How can *means* become *ends?* What is the danger with an overemphasis on *ends?* Discuss whether *ends* can ever justify *means.* Explain how the question *why?* can alter the *what?* question.

5. Define motive. Are motives important in determining the moral meaning of behavior? Give some examples. How can motives be seen as an ongoing process? Are some motives dominant or more operative than others? Give examples of this.

6. How does the question *who?* relate to the foundational moral experience? Clarify what it means to grow as a person. Why is it that what is right for one "who" might be wrong for another?

7. There seems to be an apparent problem with the phrase "some persons are worth more than others in ethical assessment." How does ethical evaluation of a particular situation disclose the worth of some individuals over others? Suppose you can save only one person in a burning building, an infant or an old woman. Whom would you save? Why? What if you know that the old woman is a Nobel laureate and is on the brink of a major breakthrough in AIDS research? How is moral worth evaluated? If artificial hearts became available in limited numbers, how would you devise criteria for distributing them? Should they be free, paid for by the government, or should they command whatever the market will bear? What justice issues are involved here?

8. Do all citizens really enjoy "equal rights"? How can the *who?* question relate to social justice?

9. The questions *when?* and *where?* refer to time and place. The *when?* question can be extremely important in cases of oil spills. *When* the clean-up operation begins is morally crucial. Give other examples. *Where* an embryo resides — frozen in a lab or growing in a womb — obviously makes a moral and legal difference.

10. Discuss the importance of *foreseeable effects* in moral evaluation. How is the future part of moral circumstances and how can effects change one's attitude toward moral reality? Explain and give some examples of moral cases where effects are *the* critical circumstance?

11. Show how the principle of proportionality relates to the responsibility that we have for good and bad effects. Discuss the morality of adoption of children by single parents stressing the foreseeable effects. Give other examples of areas where effects have moral meaning.

12. What is the nature of alternatives? Why are alternatives morally important? Explain how alternatives and effects are related. How do technological and scientific alternatives create new moral issues? An example: artificial insemination for surrogate mothering. Give other examples.

13. Explain how three forms of justice relate to the questions of alternatives and effects. Apply these questions to preferential affirmative action that seeks to break up white male monopolies.

14. How would an Ethics Committee function in a hospital setting? In business? In government? In a law firm? In a financial center? In a university?

15. Science is working on techniques for pre-selecting the sex of your child. If a successful method were developed, allowing you to conceive only the gender you choose, would it be moral? Analyze the situation using all the questions of the wheel model.

16. In what sense is it true that good ethics equals good business, good medicine, or good government?

PART THREE

Routes to Moral Truth:
Evaluating Moral Reality

8

Creative Imagination

The Evaluational Phase of Ethics...
The spokes of the wheel model represent the evaluational resources through which moral consciousness can unfold. As we saw in chapter 6, the reality-revealing questions uncover the moral circumstances. Those questions are used "to gather the evidence." In this chapter, we discuss what the spokes do to evaluate the evidence we have gathered. The spokes help us examine and judge what the reality-revealing questions uncover. They signify ways in which our pluriform consciousness can illuminate the reality unveiled by the expository process. The spokes represent the ways in which we can expand moral awareness and evaluate the moral situation. We must always remember that incompleteness and insensitivity are the bane of ethical inquiry. Comprised of both an expository *and* an evaluational phase, the method here hopes to counter these hazards. The spokes, therefore, represent *systematic concern* for the way we evaluate. They can be misused, particularly if they are uncritically accepted or if one is overemphasized to the neglect of the others. However, it is the potential positive use of all the spokes that is being stressed. The spokes give us greater moral awareness and sensitivity when uncovering the circumstances.

Ethics and the Creative Imagination...
Creative imagination is the supreme moral faculty. Through it we break out of the bondage of the current state of things and perceive new possibilities. Creative imagination offers us new insights. If creation includes discovery, moral creation implies moral discovery that enhances moral growth. The creative act can transform us into morally sensitive human beings. The process of moral discernment is not just a matter of sitting in judgment of reality as it passes by. Moral thinking at its best perceives goods that have not yet existed and brings them into being in the creative act. Creative imagination is especially allied to the reality-revealing question that deals with alternatives and with the moral growth that new alternatives may provide.

Creativity has not had much attention in ethical reflection. This unfortunate fact is partly due to the tendency to shy away from the

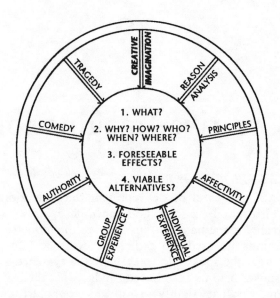

power of creative insight, a power that can easily upset the accepted and common order that we have come to rely on. Much ethical theory has been content to direct thought to what *is*, neglecting what *can* and *should be*. It seems easier to repeat past formulas and decisions than to seek new methods and answers. Creative imagination can give us new alternatives to situations that need new solutions. It can also give us a new moral orientation. Most ethical methods emphasize our rational capabilities and prefer a set way of moral judgment rather than the creative way.

Creative insight is a surprise and a challenge. There is always something unpredictable in creative intelligence. It is a leap into unsuspected insight. It opens doors we previously did not know were there. Before we discuss the place of creativity in ethics, we will touch upon its meaning and nature and briefly clarify the conditions that seem to set the stage for its moral breakthrough.

What Is the Creative Act?...
One aspect of the creative act is that it shows a likeness between two seemingly different and unrelated things; another is that it reveals a hidden order and meaning that would otherwise go unnoticed, and yet another is that its expression is new or original. In one sense, creation is an act of fusion. Professor J. Bronowski, in his book *Science and Human Values*, has given attention to the nature of the creative mind. Bronowski turns to the famous creative incident of young Newton, who saw an apple fall while he was sitting in the garden of his widowed mother. What came to Newton was not the thought that the

apple must be drawn to the earth by gravity, since that thought was older than Newton. "What struck him," Bronowski observes, "was the conjecture that the same force of gravity, which reaches to the top of the tree, might go on reaching out beyond the earth and its air, endlessly into space. Gravity might reach to the moon: this was Newton's new thought; and it might be gravity which holds the moon in her orbit." Bronowski concludes that Newton had discovered a previously hidden likeness and that creativity can be seen as "a hand reaching straight into experience and arranging it with new meaning."

Bronowski's theory is enlightening for ethics. In moral discovery there is the experience of a new unity through a recognition of previously missed likenesses. For example, take the belated discovery that women are not essentially domestic and sexual functionaries but persons with an infinity of possible meaning beyond their culturally conditioned roles. This discovery has taken longer to establish itself than the discovery of electricity, nuclear physics, or lunar gravity. After all, women and men are more alike than apples and moons, and it should have been easier to make the connections. In the recognition of the genuine and full personhood of woman, there is an insight reaching into human experience and giving it new meaning. There is a new realization of the fundamental similarity of persons, a realization that is more profound than any culturally assigned system of roles. The creative feminist is moving beyond prejudices and presenting a new and promising unity. Something similar happens as we shuffle off our biases and discover afresh the true, uncaricatured humanity of persons of other races or persons of a different sexual orientation.

Arthur Koestler has also produced an insightful study on the nature of the creative act. Like Bronowski, he stresses the discovery of hidden likenesses, but Koestler introduces a number of other important aspects. Likeness says something, but for our purposes it remains an incomplete explanation of what happens in creative moral movements. In his book *The Act of Creation*, Koestler says that the creative act "is an act of liberation — the defeat of habit by originality" and that it allows us "to attain to a higher level of mental evolution." He adds that the creative event is not unrelated to work and preparation, as when Pasteur hit upon what should have been an obvious idea of extending the notion of vaccination for smallpox to inoculation for other diseases. Pasteur's creative insight involved the blending of two elements, and he was able to see their possible linkage because he had a prepared mind. The creative insight or act, however, does not just happen as though it were determined by favorable conditions. Creative insight occurs in ways that are not easily inspected. Although inventions do influence one another, there is, nevertheless, a solitary leap taken by the creative mind in spite of all that it owes to others. No matter how hard one labors, the creative moment comes only after a period of incubation, the length of which is not in our control. One must work and then wait, with the waiting as important as the working.

Koestler's ideas are helpful for understanding breakthroughs in moral imagination. They can be applied to an example of moral creativity taken from the life of Dr. Martin Luther King, Jr. His notion of "non-violent direct action" and its use were influenced by Gandhi's teachings on *satyagraha* (a term that means a way of holding on to moral truth while resisting opposition through nonviolent means). King introduced a new urgency to the need for social and individual justice. He was responsible for revolutionary creative changes in moral America. Even though human rights and the concept of equality for all were incorporated into the U.S. Constitution, historically they were granted only to certain privileged groups. Even after the abolition of slavery, real human and civil equality was not realized by all and still has not been. To have followed through on the ideals of justice and equality would have meant condemning slavery from the very beginning of America's independence.

King's creative moral achievement and breakthrough were not unrelated to the moral insights that he received from other sources (religious, biblical, and philosophical). King's was the prepared mind that advanced the political and philosophical ideals upon which the American Constitution was formed and by which the American Revolution was motivated. In turn, King's morally creative powers helped initiate the woman's liberation movement and the struggle for rights among other minorities. Creative insight is liberating. It can prepare us for further moral growth and overcome well-entrenched habits of moral misunderstanding. It gives us an opportunity to see possible connections that otherwise would go unnoticed. Creative moral insight is an act of understanding in a new way.

In a true sense, the moral discovery of the fundamental equality of persons, including persons of other races, was a discovery not entirely unlike the discoveries of Newton and Pasteur, individuals influenced by past insights. It was not entirely like them either. The law of gravity or the practice of inoculation is one thing and the value and rights of persons, another. One should suspect that the approach of creativity to moral discovery would be as distinctive as the discovery itself. Creativity implies insight and originality. It can also imply courage and strength — characteristics that moral creativity often demands.

Creative imagination is the power to perceive the possible amid the actual and begin the process to bring the possible into being. Creativity is a promising power that is native to us. It is a power of hope and of new beginnings. Our times are not without good portents regarding the unfolding of this capacity. We admire creative talent and esteem the inventor, even though we may withdraw from creative movements that disturb or challenge our security. It is important for ethical method to emphasize that there is a creative impulse in every one of us, a desire for the new and the not yet. Since we are never satisfied only with what is, we cannot live without creative imagination. Creativity keeps persons and cultures from becoming stagnant. Sloth, on the other hand, is the attitude that counters and prevents creativity by lowering our expectations and blunting our searching instincts. The penalty of sloth is boredom that comes when we are denied newness. Boredom can send us back on the creative search. We can temporarily overcome that boredom with superficial newness, but that will soon leave us worse off. Our intellectual and volitional hunger is such that even fulfilling experiences have a bitter edge to their sweetness. We are never permanently satisfied. This fact causes within us a restlessness that becomes the wellspring of creativity. We cannot live without creative imagination. Our radical insatiability is our hope that the power of creativity will not disappear. Much more is yet to be created. The closed mind constitutes a major hazard to the liberation of the creative spirit.

Creativity is not just an intellectual ability. Its roots are in affectivity. This fact is true for all creativity but even more so for moral creativity. Creative moral imagination is born of the affections and of the humanizing power of hope. Thus it is inherently related to the foundational moral experience of the value of persons and their environment. Creative moments of moral insight reach more deeply into that experience and express more completely its meaning. Every creative advance in the application of the foundational moral experience is an affirmation of what it means to be more fully human. Moral creativity gives us new insights and helps us become aware of alternatives by offering creative solutions.

Conditions for Moral Creativity...

We cannot force creativity. We cannot command it or order it into being. What we can do is to search out the conditions that are conducive to creative achievement. To make our institutions, workplaces, and professional settings arenas of fruitful moral creativity, we can provide or encourage these preconditions of creativity. The following six factors are presented as conducive to the flowering of creative genius: *enthusiasm* (or *excitement*), *quiet passivity*, *work*, *malleability*, *kairos*, and *at-home-ness*.

Enthusiasm is the first condition for moral creativity. In fact excitement is the precondition for all success, for without it there will be no creative stirrings. Only those who are alive with humanizing love and care, with enthusiasm about the value and goodness of life will lead us across new thresholds and expand the horizons of moral consciousness. The apathetic are constitutionally disqualified. Morally creative persons can be disturbing to the uninspired and the forces of moral staidness can react violently against creative insight.

Enthusiasm is a way of feeling, an excitement that produces affect. Those affected by enthusiasm begin caring in different ways and about different things. The creative moment, however, can also be lost because excitement is not easily sustained. If moral creativity is not nourished it will pass away and the potential moral growth will vanish. Creative moral insight is perishable. But it begins with an enthused attitude about moral value. Administrators, managers, and teachers who communicate genuine enthusiasm open the door to creativity.

In apparent contradiction to the first, the second condition of creativity is *quiet passivity*. The contradiction is only apparent. Enthusiasm alone does not produce the creative act. Receptivity is an important factor, as the French philosopher Jacques Maritain points out in his work *Creative Intuition in Art and Poetry*. There is motion in artistic creation, Maritain says, the motion that puts notes on scores or color on canvas, but the creative experience "is of itself a sort of natural contemplation, obscure and affective, and implies a moment of silence and alert receptivity." Creative passivity is not to be confused with inertness or with idleness. It is an inner calm with a silence that opens us in receptivity to the powers of creative imagination. The stillness of creativity is one of the ecstatic intensities of life. No contradiction is meant here. At times there must be an inner quiet or calm that lets things happen. Surprisingly, the word "school" comes from the Greek *scole*, which means leisure. Leisure, not frenzy, allows the mind to open. Sometimes it is while we wait — or even while we sleep! — that the creative insight finds entry into our distracted minds.

Ethics could deafen itself with the noise of its own work. If we think of knowing only as something we *do* (as intellectual and discursive work) and never as something we can receive in quiet but alert passivity, then analytical and methodological thinking is the sole route to moral wisdom. But it is not. Moral truth can emerge from the nonrational depths of creativity, a valid source that is other than the rational. For creative insights, there must be some repose from the strain of the working mind. We must allow moments of rest or quiet for the possibility of creative insights. There is a message here for us who live in a society that glorifies work, the "art of doing" and the "art of achieving." We also need the "art of contemplation." We have an intellectual need for silence and receptivity. Creative moral knowledge requires more than doing. It also requires a quiet passivity. This is why the idea of the sabbatical should be part of every profession. Professions must be creative, but they will not be if genius is bottled up in busyness.

Paradoxically, the third condition for creativity is *work*. Work can prepare the mind for creative insight. If creativity involves, among other things, the discovery of hidden connections, then the more you know the more prepared you are and the better chance you have to discover these connections. Creativity includes the power to discern new possibilities within the given. Work, however, not only prepares the mind for new possibilities. It also helps prepare the disciplined attitude needed to see these possibilities through. The more attuned you are to what is, the more readied you become to see what might be. Work is part of creative readiness.

The fourth condition for moral creativity is *malleability*, the willingness to allow our moral attitudes to be shaped by the continuing growth process of the foundational moral experience. The term applies both to individual personality and to groups within a cultural setting. A placid moral milieu where no major questions are outstanding or where agreement on the values of life has gelled, will stimulate no creative movement in personal or social moral consciousness. Being unsettled by value collisions is fertile ground for growth in moral thought. Openness to moral values and the alacrity to grow in moral insight are affirmations of creative ethics. For creativity, agitation is preferable to inert serenity. Malleability helps us recognize serious value conflicts and helps us solve them in creative ways.

The fifth condition for moral creativity is what we can call *kairos*, a term rich enough to be brought in directly from the Greek. *Kairos* can be translated "time," but that is precisely why we need the Greek word intact. Time for us tends to mean chronological time, for which the Greeks had a special word: *chronos*. *Kairos*, on the other hand, means time as a moment filled with special and opportune content. It means the right moment, the right time for doing something. Obsessed as we moderns are with chronology, having organized life around the clock, it is hard to envision that time, for many of the ancients, was not primarily a matter of succession, but of content. The names for the months, for example, often described what happened in those months — the month of ripening ears, the month of flowers, the month of perennial streams, and so forth.

Kairos is the time when circumstances are such that *opportunity* is presented to us. A sense of *kairos* is a sense of knowing when the time is at hand to move beyond inadequate solutions and when the time is *ripe* for creative insights. It also knows when circumstances are not ready for the reception of the new and the creative. *Kairos* can be helpful especially at the corporate and political levels of life where decisions have massive effects for good or ill. It implies a watchful patience and a special alertness to the proper moment, to the proper timing. It is possible that the creative person will arrive, draw the creative conclusion, and be ignored. This fact can happen anywhere, in science, in politics, in business, and in all other areas of human behavior. Unfortunately, creative breakthroughs are easily missed or rejected. But *kairos* gives us a sense of knowing when to act again and even a sense of knowing how to encourage favorable conditions for the acceptance of morally creative insights.

The final condition for moral creativity can be called *at-home-ness*, the absence of alienation. The process of alienation is completely antithetical to the process of moral creation. A professional setting or any workplace marked by alienation will discourage creativity. Creation discovers and reaches out; alienation separates, turns in and away. Moral creation is a force of human meaning and integration, a force that connects the previously unconnected in the direction of greater and deeper unity. Alienation disintegrates and prevents the growth of the foundational moral experience. It is a denial of moral relationship and responsibility. It breaks down connections. If creative power is a sign of moral growth and if it enhances kinship with all that is, *at-home-ness* is one of its characteristics. To move away from moral alienation and to break down the artificial barriers that we build and revere on the basis of nation, race, sex, status, or age is to be readied for creativity. *At-home-ness* prepares us to know what only those who are and feel at-home can know. A stranger does not know *what is*, much less *what could be* in a home. At-home-ness is a prerequisite for creativity.

Creativity and Alternatives...

Moral creativity may be stimulated by the perceived value of that one alternative that would have been lost had creativity not been present. Creative imagination can propose a solution that develops a possible alternative. Thus it can enlarge moral reality and our ethical consideration of a case. When someone cares enough about a value alternative, creative imagination goes to work, for love and caring can be a source for moral creativity. Moral imagination is grounded in the affective foundational moral experience. This experience grows through moral creativity. A weakness at the level of this foundational experience can prevent creative imagination from ever expressing itself. If we do not care, we do not see alternatives. It is just that simple.

Imagination Astray...

Nothing is so sacred that it cannot be profaned. And that includes creative imagination. We can be monstrously as well as morally imaginative. The present world arsenal with its capacity to blot out all life on the planet many times over is a macabre tribute to the misuse of imagination. With all this achieved, evil imagination is not still. Far-fetched schemes are theoretically probed about more diversified modes of killing, including such things as guided tidal waves, changes effected in the electrical environment to affect brain performance, laser death rays, and almost unstoppable, computerized, robot "tanks" containing a rich repertoire of nuclear and other kill-power.

Imagination can enhance life or end it. Science in itself cannot be blamed for the perversions of our possibilities. Science is performed and implemented by human beings. It is as much a product of society as it is an influence on it. We would hope that the power of moral imagination prevails as a source of whatever humanizing good the future of persons might hold. Greater moral sensitivity is achieved through creative moral imagination. It is our primatial talent as moral beings. We can change the world into a desert or a garden. The moral choice is ours.

9

The Wisdom of the Heart

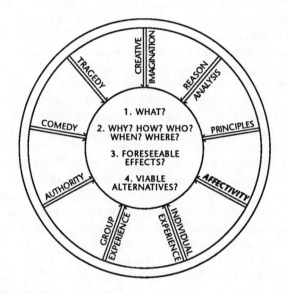

Affectivity...

All moral experience is grounded in affectivity, in the foundational moral experience of the value of persons as persons. With this spoke, however, we are not just speaking of the grounding of ethics in affectivity or feeling as we did in chapter 2. We are now speaking more specifically of how a recognition of the cognitive nature of the affections can afford a higher level of moral awareness. As it goes about addressing particular cases, ethics should take account of the value awareness that comes to us through our feeling or affection. "Affection, from intense love to mild favor," write John Dewey and James H. Tufts in their work *Ethics*, "is an ingredient in all operative knowledge, all full apprehension of the good." Affectivity, in many morally informative ways, is our rapport with the ethical world. Feeling is not totally separate from intelligence or affectivity from knowledge. Feeling is a knowing experience. It is a form of reality-contact. Failure to recognize this fact shows a flaw in moral evaluation. Incomplete awareness of how we know and of how we make moral decisions is a hazard to be avoided in ethical method. Whether we take account of them or not, our feelings arise in the face of a morally adjudicable situation. Furthermore, they arise not as neutral outbursts but as informed, evaluative reactions (positive or negative). Feelings are a cognitive reaction of knowing and they may be as mixed and contradictory as abstract and intellectual reasoning. Although feelings do not comprise the whole of moral awareness, they are important enough to be listened to. The awareness that comes through feeling is spontaneous and integral to the knowledge of morality. You may have feelings that are misleading, biased, or wrong, but they are integral and must be appreciated for what they are, and if necessary, corrected to conform to the foundational moral experience.

The following should illustrate the natural appearance of evaluative affectivity. The purpose of the example is, first, to show that feelings enter into an evaluative role with or without invitation, and, second, to suggest the positive value of having those feelings. Feeling responses, one way or another, give us an initial position on a particular subject even before we begin the needed systematic analysis that is required of holistic ethics.

In 1984 Corinne Parpalaix, a twenty-three-year-old widow, was denied access to her late husband's sperm, which had been deposited at the Center for the Study and Conservation of Sperm. Around the time Alain and Corinne Parpalaix met in 1981, he had testicular cancer and was warned that treatment could cause sterility. It was then that he decided to deposit his sperm. Alain and Corinne were married on December 23, 1983; two days later Alain died. The sperm bank, located near Paris, argued that it was obliged to refuse Mrs. Parpalaix's request because her husband had not stipulated what he wanted done with his sperm in the case of his death. On August 1, 1984, a Paris court ruled in her favor.

It is improbable that one can hear of this case and not have an immediate evaluative feeling response. Because it involves a course of action that befits or does not befit the reality of what persons are with all their unique needs and possibilities, the Parpalaix case is also a matter for moral and not just legal judgment. (Law, remember, is simply applied ethics.) Someone hearing the story for the first time would have a preliminary, tentative stance before beginning a complete ethical analysis of it. Some persons may side with Mrs. Parpalaix and be angered by the audacity of the center to hold back her late husband's sperm. Others might respond by agreeing with the decision of the center to stand by its principles. The case evokes an affective, evaluative response. In that affective response to it we are already doing ethics, though not in all the ways that a full ethical treatment would demand.

An affective response is part of the evaluative process of ethics and qualifies as a kind of moral knowledge. We should listen to our feelings. They may, at times, be smarter than our abstract reasonings. It is possible that some persons might not be able to explain or defend their affective responses, yet they have them. It is also possible that some people might go on to think about their first feelings on a moral matter and reverse their position. A negative response might, upon further reflection, yield to a positive judgment or vice versa. Any change should occur within a process that is morally informed. The change should be one from knowing to knowing better. Something happens in the affective response that must be called knowledge, and that knowledge leads us on to subsequent rational analysis that may confirm or deny the original feeling.

Affective response is not the completion of ethical decision making but the beginning, and it is not cut off from further moral intellectualization. Abstract knowledge or knowledge of certain facts may be virtually free of affectivity, but all moral knowledge is pervaded by it. Feeling, abstracting, and reasoning are interrelated in the knowing process in everyone. In sound moral insight there is not a purely affective or a purely conceptualized judgment. Conception and affection are essentially intertwined. Yet, the distinction between the two is not without a difference. Affective knowledge is not the same as conceptualized knowledge any more than experiential knowledge is the same as theoretical knowledge. A qualitative distinction to imply a total separation between affective and conceptualized knowledge has been too often and too drastically made. Affective knowing is one mode of cognitive reality contact.

Affectivity is not the only evaluational resource or spoke in the wheel model of ethical inquiry. There is no infallible feel for moral truth in any of us, but there is an initial feeling response. Moral situations evoke a *felt* response. We may call this initial response a hunch or intuition or "gut reaction," but it is evaluative and should be attended to and tested.

Feeling and Character as Conduits of Truth...

There is an intrinsic relationship between our character and our affections, between who we are and what we choose, love, and do. The reality of character is basic to an understanding of the moral life. Character is the embodiment of our moral orientation and affections. It is the moral thrust of our personalities, which are given their direction from our moral history and from the values we nourish and from the decisions we make. Morally we are what we do and fail to do. Character refers to this fact. It is the kind of person we have chosen to be. Character is not a superficial disposition or passing emotion. It is a substantial moral development from the values with which we identify through our choices.

Because character reflects the roots and moral center of the personality, it has a certain stability and expectation. Atypical behavior is questioned. It is seen as "uncharacteristic." Sudden and major shifts in character are not to be looked for. A ruthless political operative who suddenly becomes morally transformed and religiously fervid is duly and properly suspect for a time. Character involves personality direction that has been established over a long period. It affects our way of seeing reality.

Character has considerable momentum and cannot go immediately into reverse. Obviously, there is no one who has a purely good or bad character. We are all amalgams of values and disvalues. However, certain overall moral traits are discernible in persons. We are instinctively alert to these traits or characteristics when "sizing people up." We do not perceive persons as a page filled with unconnected dots. We find connections and patterns, enough to make some judgment on "the kind of person" they are and the kind of thing they are likely to do. What we glimpse is called character. It is a factor in moral knowledge. People in business and the professions are constantly judging moral character. They are well advised to think about what it means.

We may intellectually know about moral values without their being a part of our character or of our affections. Affectivity engenders character and offers a fuller experience of moral knowledge, an experience that goes beyond abstract intellectuality. What we merely know abstractly we can be detached from because it allows for distance. What we love we become through our affections. Love is a unitive force and the basis of moral meaning. The foundational moral experience is an affective response to moral value and the source of moral character. A good character is a source of moral wisdom. Aristotle advised us to trust the judgments of good people, i.e., of those who have a good character. The unjust person might be a whiz at ethical theories of justice but his or her knowledge of justice is flawed by a lack of affective experience. A good character makes us not just *knowers* of moral truth, but *connoisseurs*. Our characters are lenses through which we perceive reality.

On Delight and the Sense of Profanation...

Your delights show us who you are. In the phenomenon of delight and in its opposite, the sense of profanation, we have two of the most perceptible manifestations of the cognitive capacity of affectivity and character. If we delight in the acts that pertain to a certain moral value, we know that this value has woven its way into our character. But if we perform certain moral acts begrudgingly, we know the opposite is true; our delights do not rest there. That which is morally good should resonate delightfully in the person who is morally sensitive.

In delight there is an affective response to a particular value option that is experienced as congenial and suitable and in accord with one's moral orientation. A response of delight amounts to an endorsement of that which is perceived and implies an enveloping awareness of value that we enjoy in ourselves. That which is delightful we want to enjoy fully. If we delight in the value of persons and the values that enhance all life, we tend to absorb them into the tonality of our moral consciousness. Delight weaves its object into our beings. Situations involving those values will touch on our delights and affections. Even with all the help we need and get from clever reasoning in assessing these situations, feeling, too, will instruct us and direct our reach for the truth. The just person delights in justice and has a "feel" for just solutions.

The sense of profanation is the nether side of delight. It is the shock and withdrawal that we feel when the value of life is debased. If persons are valued as persons, their violation in any way, as we pointed out in chapter 1, can evoke the feeling of profanation. As was true with the feeling of delight, the feeling of profanation extends to the worlds of nature and art. Sometimes that which is valuable is taken for granted, and only after the sense of profanation that follows upon violation or destruction might we become sensitive to the delight that we in our apathy had missed. The emerging ecological awareness that is taking place internationally might come to illustrate this point. We used nature and subdued it abusively — and we still do. As shock begins to register on our obtuse consciousness, there are signs of reawakening affections and enthusiasm for the earth that bore and sustains us. If this is more than lightly romantic and ephemeral, a new capacity to delight in the richness of the good earth might be born of the new and shocking awareness of eco-catastrophe.

When Affective Knowledge Is Disdained...

Cognitive awareness is not limited to intellectual knowledge alone. As we have been discussing, there is also affective awareness that can cradle initial moral insight. Affective knowledge has often been rejected in ethical theory. There is even a wider cultural denial of affectivity that is discernible in the cultural disparagement of things associated with women. We have tended to associate the intuitive and affective insight with women. The lack of the role of affectivity has a damaging effect on ethical thought. More generally, ethics has gone forward with heartless head in command. There would, of course, be havoc if headless heart were in charge of human affairs. But there is a greater capacity for cruelty in heartless head.

Ethics seeks the alliance of head and heart. Those ingenious military planners who cooly and cleverly calculate in terms of megadeaths are an example of the perils of unfeeling mind. Those who would lyrically imply that politics could be done without reference to the category of power would be an example of headless heart. Heart and head together would be in pursuit of expressions of power that can be effective without resort to slaughter. In moral persons, head and heart unite. Affections keep us close to the flesh and find the reality of persons beneath abstractions and statistics. This knowledge is the affective contribution to the living mind in pursuit of values.

How Practical Affective Knowledge?...

One reason modern ethics has not been attentive to affective evaluation is that it is no simple matter to say precisely how one incorporates affectivity into a systematic ethical treatment. It is a more manageable task to speak of moral principles because there is a lot we can get a grip on. We can discuss the history of principles, the relationship of the general to the exceptional, the meaning of universalizability, and so on. With principles, there is the reassuring feeling that this is indeed workable turf. In addressing particular cases, we can summon relevant principles to test their applicability, and, in so doing, we can have a good sense of knowing what we are about. But how do we summon affectivity when attempting to analyze the moral import of a situation? Should we repair to a meditation room and allow our feelings to play upon the cases at hand and then bring back a report to the table where the hard ethical analysis is going on?

These questions, of course, are misconceived. In setting up the wheel model of ethical method, we are not implying that all the evaluational processes and resources signified by the spokes can be similarly employed in ethical inquiry and in every case. Two spokes yet to be discussed, for example, relate to humor and tragedy. Obviously, one could not do ethics by reasoning and analyzing for a while, by applying principles for a while, and then by looking for the comic side of the matter. There are times when a comic evaluation would show insensitivity or times when it would not be germane.

What we are stressing in this method is that the unfolding of moral consciousness is pluriform. Sensitivity to the moral dimension of existence is not achieved only through reasoning or through the application of principles or even through the exercise of creative imagination. An ethics that stresses only one or some of the evaluative processes is partial. Unfortunately, such partiality has been a common failing in ethics. A complete ethics should seek to develop an awareness of all the ways in which consciousness awakens to moral reality. Some of the ways are more easily describable processes. Some may have no particular relevance to certain cases. Some will point us more toward the background and presuppositions of our thought. And some will involve a bit of all these aspects and more. How, then, does affectivity operate in ethical analysis? It is necessary to be aware of the fact that our evaluation *is* affectively as well as intellectually actuated. If we assumed that our ethical thinking proceeds with limpid and undiluted intellectuality, we would not only be naive but, worse yet, the easy prey of untested affective forces that can easily be partial and biased in their sway. Affective orientation is not foolproof. Just as a lawyer wants to know the vested interest of a client, so must we be aware of where our feelings are, where they are pulling us and why. The vested interest that affects our thinking may make us *more* or *less* drawn to the truth. The morally wise person is one who learns from the heart that feeling has its own insights...and prejudices.

Uncritical thought undermines good ethics. Thus, whoever denies the cognitive side of affectivity will not be proceeding critically. Full moral judgment, however, cannot be made from feelings alone. Feelings tell you something, but not everything. One may need to step back from feelings and pause, and then make a moral judgment while remembering the insights that feelings have given. Misconceptions about the potential negative dimensions of affectivity could only have an unhappy yield along the way of ethical inquiry. No system of ethics can ignore this fact. Bigots, after all, speak from the heart. They are surely *feeling* people. Fanaticism, too, is an offspring of heightened affectivity. Adolf Hitler is alleged to have said, "I think with my blood." Affections unaided by discipline and analytical activities of working reason can lead to moral chaos. As we pointed out in the opening of chapter 8, the spokes are to be trusted and distrusted because they can be used and misused. Affectivity, along with all the other spokes, must be tested and balanced.

Full ethical inquiry must take advantage of the positive yield of affectivity. In studying particular issues in ethics, our antennae should be alerted to the wisdom of the heart, which can serve as a corrective for reason gone amuck. But sometimes when we look for the wisdom of the heart, we will hear contradictory answers. The heart, like the intellect, does not specialize in unequivocal conclusions. Here, as in all situations of disagreement, a comprehensive ethics wants to hear both sides to find the part of truth that each may be presumed to contain.

All this may sound abstract and unpractical. It is not. Parents often use the wisdom of the heart. There are no blueprints for rearing a child. There are no tidy rules that tell you when leniency or severity might be more cruel. Nurses responding to the needs of seriously ill patients often follow their feelings with all the experience those feelings contain. This is not irrational, although any decisions made in a unique or emergency situation should be subjected to reasoned analysis later. However, we encounter circumstances where our intuitive feelings, educated as they are by experience (including past reasoning), are our only guide for the moment. It is wise, therefore, to be aware of our feelings and to discuss them. They are a crucial component of our moral equipment. Nurses, physicians, journalists, administrators, and all others in roles of authority and influence should know and experience the value of our affective "instincts."

Culture and Feelings...

Sensitivity to affective evaluation is also essential in the ethical analysis of cultural trends. The heart has a sense of direction. Often it can catch the scent of trouble or opportunity. In affectivity, there is, as in creativity, a future referent. We feel for the future we cannot see. We can analyze the past and the causal factors operating in the present so as to make useful but tentative judgments about the kinds of effects that might continue into the future. The analysis could all be a dominantly "intellectual" enterprise, but the heart seems to have special prerogatives for conducting its own probes into the future and it should be a part of our morally analytical efforts. Affectivity can open us to greater moral creativity and discovery, often needed resources in ethical discourse. A professional atmosphere or workplace that suppresses feeling also suppresses creativity.

At times we need affective relief when dealing with ethical questions. For instance, affectivity can balance our attitude toward the appeal of expert knowledge by agitating our blind reliance on the expert. The expert, though often needed, can be one of the more oppressive authorities in the modern world. (When we discuss the spoke that relates to *authority* in chapter 10, we will return to this.) Although the expert may be a temporary cure for vertigo in the midst of abounding complexity, there is a hazard here. Because the expert has privileged knowledge, it would seem rash and immodest to question this person. He or she has done work that you have not and bears credentials that you do not have. Docility, then, would seem to be the expert's due and the expert could easily become a tyrant. Expertise, however, is not infallible. It is borne by people who have their own presuppositions, their own unasked questions, and their own vested interest in the conclusions they have already taken a stand on. They can be as wrong as they can be impressive.

The power of the expert can be relativized in two important ways. First, by questioning. No expertise is beyond questions. And second (a way that may inspire the first) is by using common sense or intuition. This kind of thinking is richly endowed with affectivity and includes the incipient intellectual insight that has caught a glimpse of a solution that is not yet grasped. This insight-affect, if we may so phrase it, gives us a feel for moral truth and has its own valid credentials. The affections keep us close to earth and thus less vulnerable prey to abstractions. Affective response is an important resource to have, as long as it is not thought to be self-sufficient and the end of the thinking process.

Affectivity and Principles...

A final word on our affective approach to truth relates to principles. Ethics is best seen as an art/science. Like art, ethics cannot be done simply by following a method of rules. Guidelines or principles play an indispensable role, but they do not of themselves yield moral discernment. However well instructed we are by moral principles, there is a certain point when one's humane sense of the personal and contextual factors of a case attains crucial importance. Rules and regulations cannot tell you how to approach someone who not only needs your help but also your confidence. Principles and the experience of others can be passed on and can be helpful, but only to a degree. The final judgment of the fitting way to proceed in moral cases will be based on affect, on a feeling response to what a particular situation requires. When it comes to the basic ethical necessities, such as contextual sensitivity and delicacy, a sense of timing and opportuneness, we move beyond rules and principles and into the realm of affective perception.

If reality is process, a moral decision involves a step into that process at the fitting and most potentially fruitful time. To make a moral decision on abstract grounds alone would be to operate at only one level of our cognitional capacity. To know the right time, the *kairos*, calls for both the genius of the intellect and the genius of the heart. Sound ethics knows that the heart is wise in its own fashion.

10

Reason and Reliance

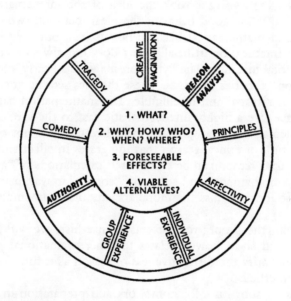

Reason and Reliance...
The next two significant modes of moral evaluation are *reason and analysis* and *authority*. Reason and authority function throughout all the human processes of thought. In our ethical method, these two spokes, like *individual* and *group experience*, are taken together. They provide a system of checks and balances. One is not meant to exclude the other. All the evaluational resources, of course, are interrelated but some more so than others. Here we will show first how the spoke on *reason and analysis* contributes to ethics and then we will discuss the spoke on *authority*.

Reason and Analysis...
Reason is as broad as human life. We can see it at work everywhere from science to poetry, though with varying degrees of ascendance and in varying forms. Although our reasoning process should be qualified by

the challenge we address, reasoning always means thinking thoroughly and clearly. In ethics, one would rightly expect reason to take on and reflect the nature of moral experience. The ancients saw *recta ratio*, right reason, as the guiding light of ethics. But if it were to function in the same way as it does in other areas of experience, such as in mathematics, where reason can reach high levels of abstractness, it would mean that moral experience is not distinctive.

The Pythagoreans of ancient Greece believed that numbers and proportions constituted the basis of reality. This was their dominant metaphor. Since our thought bears the marks of our metaphors, we find that the Pythagoreans took the idea of the mathematical *mean* and, in ethics, made good behavior the mean between two extremes. Metaphor and mathematical bias are not useless, but they introduce a certain abstractness or artificiality that does not always meet the demands of moral meaning. The Pythagoreans were an early influence on "right reason" theories in ethics. These theories see the good only as that which is rational and intelligible. The mathematical basis of the Pythagoreans gave a highly intellectualistic cast to the idea of reason. But a mathematical paradigm falls short because it is not conducive to a conception of ethical reason that integrates intellect and affectivity. Cold, naked reason can be cruel. Cold calculations of "acceptable levels of unemployment" and counts of "sorties" in war may be mathematically sound but miss the moral tragedy of the unemployed and the dead.

To explain the proper role of reason in ethics, we will list some of its tasks and show how it relates to other evaluational processes. We will also clarify the distinctiveness of reason as it functions in the mind of the ethicist.

There is no substitute for homework and preparation in ethics or in any field. This kind of labor is reason's task. Reason has more to do with perspiration than with inspiration. It is not content to wait in passive intensity but throws itself into the task of truth-finding. *Reason is working intelligence*. Thus, we combine it with analysis to emphasize its laboring function. Analysis means to break up, or to break open. Early impressions in ethics and elsewhere come to us largely in undifferentiated globs. Reason and analysis break them up and sort them out so that we can know what we are talking about. Often the task is mammoth but always essential. We can quickly see that this spoke on *reason and analysis* relates especially to the *what* question in the hub of the wheel model. If you are going to talk about the moral advantages of affirmative action, you had better know what it is and how it affects the labor pool. You had also better know all the objections to it. *If you do not face the objections to your position, you do not know your position*. Reason struggles with all the objections. There was a period in the Middle Ages when it was felt that the best way to know your position is to look first at all the objections to it that you can find. There was wisdom in that tactic.

Reason has its work cut out for it in every area of moral experience. Among its critical tasks are: to find and compare ethically meaningful data; to search for the unasked questions; to test the regnant authorities before which minds may be playing dead; to cope with the inevitable partiality of our knowledge; to jog the lazy memory; to fight the allure of too facile consensus; to break the stranglehold of habituation; to check our myths and other filters; to solve the conflict between and among principles; and to tend to the reformulation and correction of principles in view of new experience and moral insight. In a word, reason works to be critical and to fight the superficiality that is the fruit of homework undone. Reason can also be the forebear of creativity. It is not pure luck that fully explains a creative contribution. Hard-working reason and analysis are often the preparing factors for creative insight. Reason can serve to prepare the mind by bringing critical thought to the discovery of shallow consensus and ideological blinders. It can provide the research and the solid information base that are the prerequisites for creativity. Reason must also make sure that the mind stays in process and that it does not take its ease by pretending that reality is immobile.

Reason and Affection...

Unlike all other disciplines and studies, ethical reason is distinctly in pursuit of moral values — those which touch upon what we are as persons. In the previous spoke, we discussed how values are appreciated affectively. We do not reason about person-related values like we reason about mathematical theorems. We are affectively engaged from the start. Our vested interests, our characters, our mood and emotional state *always* influence moral reasoning. This is not necessarily bad. Well and sensitively tuned affections are a component of moral wisdom.

Reasonable or Rationalistic...

Reason has two verbal relatives that are scarcely on speaking terms. They are *reasonable* and *rationalistic*. One has felicitous connotations, the other does not. Reasonable, the good relative, is not just an adjective that relates to reason. It has a broader meaning and is instructive about the role and nature of reason. To be called reasonable is a compliment. No one would want to be considered anything else. Wrong, maybe, but never unreasonable! "Reasonable" connotes an openness to reality and ideas, balance and thoroughness. In a notable way, this sense of reasonableness emerges in the "reasonable man" criterion employed in court decisions. Such usage exemplifies jurisprudential confidence in the reasoning mind and in the category of reasonableness. It amounts to saying that the reasonable is equivalent to the good, the legal, the proper. The implication is that what is reasonable is moral. The word "reason" does not bear all these connotations in general parlance. But it should bear them in a thoughtful ethics. Reasonable, on the other hand, does not always imply the serious work that reason does. With the right qualifications and with the full meaning of *ethical* reason in view, it is possible to say that the reasonable (i.e., morally informed reason) and the good are synonymous, an idea that can be found in certain "natural law" theories of ethics.

"Rationalistic," the other verbal relative of reason, cannot easily be caught in a precise definition, but it implies that reality can adequately be grasped by and confined to our rational abilities. Sole concentration on reason turns rationalistic. In an Irish colloquial expression, rationalistic thinking is "entirely too smart." It is reason shorn of its necessary modesty and limits. Rationalistic thinking in moral matters is cut off from collaborative affectivity and it can easily become heartless head. Rationalism is too fastidious and neat, prone to tidiness even when the truth is sloppy. Rationalistic views are not sufficiently hedged by a sense of mystery and by the modesty that mystery engenders. The hubris of rationalism is to think that the mind can take the full measure of the real. The rationalistic is overconfident reason. Reason can be misused in moral evaluation, even though it always presupposes hard work. Sartre's words are again relevant: the worst evil of which we are capable is to treat as abstract that which is concrete. Rationalistic thinking does just that. We may lose the good of persons in abstractions.

Rationalistic notions of "efficiency" can smother the good of persons. Rationalistic theories of sexuality, for example, have become so removed from sexual reality as to label such actions as masturbation to be always wrong. Similarly, rationalistic reasoning has defined sex in exclusively heterosexual terms, thereby missing the possibility of wholesome and humane homosexual relationships. Rationalism devises tidy schemes and denies validity to whatever does not fit into its artificial grids.

Because it can be abused and because it is work, reason can be less revered at times and can find itself in recess. Our age is inclined to bypass the laborious horizontal explorations of ethical reason and to move by a vertical stroke to hasty moral conclusions. The philosopher E. W. Kluge is of the opinion that "if there is one thing that characterizes the current moral scene, it is the abandonment of deliberate reason in favor of unreasoned personal preference." Such an approach leaves us at the mercy of whimsey even though whimsey may defend itself in terms of conscience. Ethics in any age must defend the proper role of reason, and especially in an age when reason recedes before the impervious emotions of personal opinion.

Authority and the Art of Reliance...

After all the praises of reason and analysis have been sounded, it is still probable that most of the moral conclusions we make are not the result of a reasoning process but are directly due to the influence of someone we admire or love, or to the influence of traditional and accepted wisdom. Principles and other teachings that we have never questioned, the pressures of society and customs, influence us through the *authority* they contain. Authority is a formidable influence and power over us. Its force can direct our behavior and govern the moral decisions we make. Reliance on authority of one kind or another is probably the most common way of moral evaluation. We all have our own authorities and even those who feel highly independent and liberated are not immune. We are more docile than we suppose.

Through our cognitional experience we may come to understand and appropriate what we accept on authority. Acceptance, however, without critical examination is an unfortunate commonplace. Sometimes we rely on authority to avoid making our own moral decisions. It seems less burdensome to us to devolve our moral responsibility upon those in authority. But authority can attempt to control the thoughts and actions of others without giving convincing or conclusive arguments, and it can defend positions that need correction. It could simply be maintaining a taboo. Authority must be open to moral growth. If it insists on its positions regardless of new moral insight, it can become a brutal force. Because authority can be wrong, it should be open to change when new moral insights emerge. It may be holding on to ideals that were never morally sound or to principles that are no longer tenable or applicable. Some moral positions and principles may be based on originally misplaced values, prejudiced opinions, and faulty reasons that have taken on the appearance of respectability through tradition. Moral wisdom is a process of growth. What was once held may not with the same force be held today.

Reliance on authority in doing ethics, then, might seem at first to be a problem, a defection from the work of intelligence. However, in presenting authority as one of the evaluational processes of ethical method, we are viewing it as a positive resource for understanding. Like all the other evaluational resources illustrated by the spokes of the wheel model, authority can be used or abused. The study of authority is fraught with some special difficulties. There are times in our individual lives and in our society that we may indulge in the illusion of thinking ourselves free and independent of all authority. Let us first see reliance on authority as a fact of life and then move on to see its potential for use and misuse in ethics.

Types of Authority . . .

Persons, even sophisticated ones, are conspicuously prone to "buy a bill of goods" with uncritical acceptance. There are a number of perennial authority sources from whose sway none of us entirely escapes. Let us look at some of the more potent forms of authority that operate in our social world, namely, peer authority, expertise, religious and crypto-religious authority (including nationalistic authority), tradition, and charisma.

First, there is the domineering authority of peer group. It is no easy task to stand apart from its dictates. What the peer group does among young and old is to establish an evaluational orthodoxy from which it takes courage and strength of mind to depart. Staying within it is not without its alluring satisfactions. It seems that everyone wants to belong to a club with all its rules, regulations, and amenities. There is an identity that comes through the peer group. Moral value positions are closely linked to our sense of identity and to the emotions that go along with it. Dissenters against established positions are perceived as threats and outcasts. Hence, the peer group consensus will be re-enforced by a number of sanctions ranging from excommunication to ridicule. This phenomenon of peer group authority is as visible in countercultural groups as it is in the board rooms.

Second, the perennial authority that has taken on a revolutionary new force in an increasingly complicated and data-loaded world is the *expert*. Clearly the expert is an essential authority in a time when the idea of universal knowledge is seen as chimeric. The expert is the only relief from swelling complexity. The problem with experts is that they can become oracles and command even our common sense to recede before the prestige of their special qualifications. But experts are not beyond questions and accountability, for they, too, can have vested interests and their knowledge can be biased and misleading. Some estimate that one-third of all surgery done in the United States is unnecessary. Sooner than get second and third opinions, people bow to the expert and accept an unnecessary invasion of their bodies. In some ways expertise has gone mechanical in our day with the advent of the computer. The computer adds the attractiveness of apparently unalloyed objectivity.

Third, authority always operates powerfully in religious and crypto-religious contexts. Wherever the aura of the sacred accrues, there is a tendency for critical judgment to give way to awe. Since moral experience brings us into contact with the phenomenon of sacredness, one could expect religiously tinged authorities to operate here. The major

religions have been active in assuming an authoritative and divinely in-
spired role in matters moral. We find authoritative moral teachings and
scriptures in most religions: the Vedas of the Hindus, the Koran and
the Hadith of the Muslims, the Dharma of the Buddhists, the Tanak
and Talmudic writings of the Jews, and the scriptures of the Christians. Religions meet a socially felt need in spelling out the meaning
and shape of the good life.

What is important to note is that much that is numinous in character is located within the apparently secular; this fact is crypto-religion.
Supposedly secular attitudes found in nationalism and patriotism have
been recognized as "full of Gods," in the words of the ancient Thales.
A nation is no merely pragmatic association of persons but, rather, a
social entity endowed with a sacred mystique that can evoke complete
devotion from its citizens even to the point of the "supreme sacrifice"
of their lives. National heroes assume sainted roles. The foundational
documents and constitutions of nations acquire a sacred quality. Official communiqués are often accepted by the press as scripture. Those
who hold high office achieve an authority that has hallowed overtones.
In classical times the national leader or emperor was thought to be
divine. (There was a slight modification of this when the Emperor Au-
relian renounced his claim to be a human God and declared himself
with only slightly less pride to be no more than God's vicegerent on
earth.)

In the modern state the sacrality of the leader is more muted,
though it shows through in inaugural ceremonies and in the protocol
that attend officials of state. We have not yet outgrown the sacralized
tribe. Sacralized civil authority is extant. It is visible in caricature form
in the "super-patriot" whose zeal could only be described within the
categories of religious devotion. It also can appear in more subtle form
in the conceptualization of citizenship. Religious authority, whether implicit and crypto or explicit and denominational, remains a major force
in the valuations of both private and political ethics today.

Fourth, *tradition* is another common authority. Tradition breeds
familiarity, and the familiar is likely to seem reliable and true. The
"traditional" has some likely claims to reliability, since that which has
stood the test of time is probably not without some merit. However,
since error can become as traditional as truth, this authority too must
be tested.

Fifth and last, *charisma* is a widely influential form of authority. The
term need not be limited to the magnetic qualities of political figures,
but it can refer to the personality strengths that are present more or
less in almost everyone by virtue of which we can sway and influence
others. In any group, charisma will function and will exert influence on
the group members. Charisma has many ingredients. The attractiveness

of persons, the attitudes and confidence they project, the emotions they engender, and so forth, all give persons influence or charisma. Achievement lends charisma, as does the mere fact of being famous. Nations can gain charisma because of inspirational achievements or simply because of their technological prowess. The forces that generate charisma might be worthy or irrelevant. For this reason, a sensitive ethics must alert persons to the presence of charismatic influences in their thought processes. Charisma can function negatively or positively, but the point here is that it is a pervasive, persuasive force where persons interact and evaluate. No workplace or professional setting is without the ambivalent power of charisma.

Authority and Personal Responsibility...

As we can see, authority functions in myriad forms. The human mind accepts on authority ethical positions that it has not thought through. Yet, it seems that all forms of traditional authority are coming under attack in our present-day society. That there has been a change is undeniable. Authority, today, must show that it is trustworthy and that it promotes the good. Authority must be earned and evaluated and proved authentic. It does not come *ex officio*. There is progress here because there is a slight move away from magical forms of oracular authority that prevent moral discussion and moral growth.

Excessive dependence on authority is a one-sided approach to ethics, an approach that ultimately represents a despair of our capacity to know. However, in an integral approach to ethics, there is a healthy reliance on authority. The authority found in principles or in persons with experience may enlighten others. And sometimes a person who grows in moral experience will come to realize the wisdom of authority.

Proper reliance on authority is both a practical necessity and a community-building form of trust. Dependence on authoritative sources is required by our finitude. Complexity is expanding exponentially and, as a result, knowledge is more specialized. The dream of comprehensive knowledge has passed and any attempt to retrieve it would condemn us to superficiality and frustration. But reliance on authority must be critical and not naive. Since authorities can disagree, they must be tested and seen to be credible and trustworthy. We should always be aware of the authorities influencing us. The spoke on authority represents one of the many evaluational processes by which we grope toward the truth. It is not the only one. When possible the mind should not rest with accepting something as true on the authority of another. It should attempt to know what it accepts. Just because a committee has been assigned to study some subject, that does not mean that they have become infallible. The whole committee may have become sidetracked or dragged into uncritical "groupthink."

Although authority should not do our thinking, one of its positive roles is pragmatic. We often need the help of others and in accepting authority we get that help from those sources that we judge reliable. Because authority is a personalizing and community-building form of trust, there is a deeper meaning to it. The tendency we have to rely on the opinions of others is more than pragmatic. It is also a manifestation of our social nature. In a matter of merely technical expertise, the trust element will be less important than the indicators of genuine knowledgeability. But when authority functions at a more personal level, a process of trust is in effect. Valid moral authority functions only in an atmosphere of trust. Good leaders and managers and teachers are those who *earn* trust and don't just assume and demand it.

Authority in moral matters operates powerfully within a matrix of personal exchange. We will trust the value inclinations of persons whom we find worthy. Contrariwise, those factors that hinder personal relationships also block the functioning of authority. The deeper and fuller a relationship is, the greater will the individuals in that relationship become authorities to one another. Friendship breeds trust in the value orientation. Even if we rarely think of it, a true friend is a moral authority.

Acceptance of authority is not just an impersonal acceptance of a source of information. It is also a personal response to the personal source of that authority and a favorable assessment of the moral qualities involved. Thus it is a socializing act. Authority is not an alien intrusion on the autonomy of a rational person. Rather, it is part of a system of reliance and trust that increases our contact with persons and intensifies our relationships. This reality is a normal part of developing moral consciousness. The inability to accept authority influences is not only a social and psychological problem; it is a problem in ethics. Yet, total reliance on authority shows diminished moral growth and a lack of personal responsibility.

Concluding Reason/Analysis and Authority...

Reason and reliance on moral authority, though apparently as antithetical as independence and dependence, are conjoined in the service of moral truth. Each is a way in which our pluriform consciousness seeks attunement with the moral good as it emerges in the swirl of social historical existence. Reason and authority are both broad concepts. The fuller meaning of each for ethics will be seen in the elaboration of other parts of this ethical method. Each is a check against the other and must be seen as operating in a balance for greater moral truth. Reason is involved in the whole expository phase of ethics and is a collaborative force in most of the evaluative processes. Authority operates in a number of ways aside from those mentioned in this section. Principles, for example, come to us with the authority of cultural acceptance and they are often religiously and legally fortified. The discussion of *group experience* will illustrate the ways in which the individual is drawn into the moral patterns of the group. Here the attempt has been to show, as any exposition of ethical method must, how the mind should pursue moral truth through the work of reason and the virtue of reliance.

11

The Nature
of Moral Principles

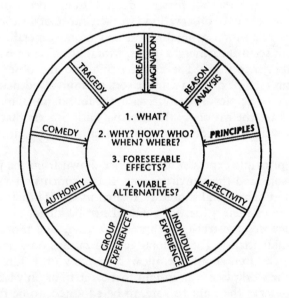

Principles: Consistency and Surprise...
Moral principles are intellectual generalizations containing value judgments that have been shaped from our collective and personal experience. They offer a perspective of moral wisdom and attempt to meet human needs. Principles are the voice of history and the moral memory of a people. Without them we would be like amnesiacs with no sense of past experience or moral history. Although principles do not give us a blueprint of the present or the future, they can broaden our outlook, offer depth, and make us more sensitive and less vulnerable in ethical discourse. They give us an added moral perspective.

Whether they are the collective moral experience of our forebears or the fruits of our own experience of moral value, principles are culturally based propositions or generalizations about what befits or does not befit the behavior of human beings. Principles can be positive (Keep promises) or negative (Do not kill); very generic and broad (Do good and avoid evil) or quite specific (Do not cheat). The terms "precepts," "laws," "norms," and "rules" can be used interchangeably and as synonyms for *principles*, since they refer to the same moral reality. The applicability and elasticity of a principle relate both to its form and to the moral circumstances.

Moral principles are not just empirical or scientific generalizations of the sort one finds outside ethics. In physics, for example, principles about the properties of gases can be based on uninvolved observation. It is a principle of physics that metal, when heated, expands. We are into more profound experiences of truth, however, when we state the moral principle that all persons deserve due process under law. That is not an obvious observation. In fact, most of history missed it entirely. It is a moral generalization and moral generalizations are different from scientific generalizations. Moral principles are as unique as moral experience itself. The experiencing and the observing that produce them are not of the scientific sort of uninvolved detachment. Because moral principles are derivatives of the foundational moral experience, they have their roots in the affective faith process that grounds all ethics as well as in reflection, observation, memory, and creative imagination.

A moral principle expresses an influence drawn from the perceived value of persons and their environment. It is a conclusion about how persons should behave and should be treated in view of their perceived value. Because of their value, they should not be killed, exploited, or deceived; they deserve truth, fidelity, and caring, due process under law, and confidentiality. These moral generalizations only dawn on us slowly. That children should be allowed to grow up before they are forced into the workplace is an insight that came to us only lately. That all persons deserve the right to vote, to be educated, to be freely represented by an attorney if they are poor, are only modern discoveries. Morally, we get smart very slowly.

Principles are the voiced specifications of the foundational moral experience, and to have moral authenticity, they must reflect that experience. Principles relate to creative imagination, since they preserve in reflective and propositional form the creative insights of a people or a group or a person on what does or does not enhance our moral evolution toward fuller humanity. They are the creative insights that have achieved tenured status in a culture. Moral principles are distinctive, as is moral imagination, when compared, for example, to technological imagination. The difference is qualitative and points us beyond the quantifiable to the deeply personal and human roots of ethics.

The Personal and Empirical Roots of Ethics...
Principles do not just occur out of nothing. They are reflective responses to the moral value within human experience. They meet human needs and situations. Moral principles have a contextual and empirical basis and sometimes they meet the needs of very specialized situations. For example, at one time it was a principle among the Eskimos to practice a kind of socially motivated geriatric suicide. To relieve critical population pressures in the face of severely limited food supply, some of the older folks would resignedly go off to die on an ice floe. In the absence of any alternatives, this principle could be judged a tragic but moral practice. Within their specific moral circumstances, it was the best they could do to survive as a people, since the whole race might have perished without this practice. One could not, of course, rip this moral principle out of that specific empirical context in which it might have been temporarily defensible and say that it would be a good practice for others to whom more benign alternatives are available. Principles derive from circumstances, and circumstances make moral reality distinguishable and specific.

Not all principles have such a narrow empirical base as this particular one of the Eskimos. Some principles are relevant to any context imaginable. The prohibition of rape, lying, and violence are among these, as are the positive principles that urge us to revere and nourish life. But these principles too were learned in concrete circumstances, and they cannot be applied except in dialogue with the realities of the concrete order. In circumstances of self-defense, the very desire to revere and nourish life may press us to kill when no other alternatives for the protection of the innocent are available. The ethical principle of licit killing in self-defense springs from that reality. *In fact, ethics can be seen as a dialogue conducted by the moral agent between the moral meaning found in principles and that found in the unique circumstances of the case.* Principles are thus tied to the empirical order by reason of their origin and their application.

Deep down in good principles there is contact with the sanctity of life. Although principles may be skewed or may be reflective of outmoded data and myths, we should not part from them without due process. If we find in our cultural reservoirs principles urging the counterproductivity of violence, the responsibility to comfort a dying person without hastening death, or principles that affirm the value of compassion and truth-telling, we should reflect deeply upon their counsel before leaving them for a more morally valuable alternative. Only one who is well aware of the significance of principles has the moral sensitivity to depart from them safely.

The Quest for Universals: Trying to Make Principles Absolute...
There is a tendency at times to universalize moral principles or to make individual experience applicable to all. There is, of course, some basic wisdom in the attempt to universalize. For one thing, it makes us less liable to caprice and self-serving rationalizations. Universalizability means that moral decisions are not simply intuitive and ad hoc. Principles arise out of moral experience and can in turn be applied to similar experiences. If you conclude that you ought to do *x* in circumstances A-B-C, you should be willing to universalize your insight by saying that anyone like you in circumstances A-B-C should do the same thing.

The very influential German philosopher Immanuel Kant can be used as an example of one who has greatly stressed the universalizability of principles. In "On a Supposed Right to Lie from Altruistic Motives," Kant wrote: "Truthfulness in statements which cannot be avoided is the formal duty of an individual to everyone, however great may be the disadvantage accruing to himself or to another." If you think about Kant's statement, you will realize that he is attempting to universalize one principle over all others and to make it absolutely applicable to every situation. Very simply, Kant would not be the man you would want to stand between you and someone intent on murdering you — at least if Kant knew where you were. Affectivity and feeling are minimized in Kant's theoretical view of principles and moral reality. Principles conflict with one another at times and some are more morally relevant than others. Cut off from empirical considerations and affectivity that would help us plumb the moral meaning in situations, Kant builds a grid into which he would fit reality willy-nilly. Reality is just too diverse and surprising to be so circumscribed. Common sense and good ethics tell us that we make distinctions when there are differences. Different situations can point up the limits of principles.

Unwittingly, Kant illustrates why it would be better to use the term "generalization" rather than "universalization" in reference to the applicability of principles. By making reason the a priori author of its own principles and by refusing to lean "in the least on empirical grounds" (Kant's terms in *Foundations of the Metaphysics of Morals*), Kant pushes principles too far. He even said you would have to tell the truth to someone intent on murder regarding the location of the intended victim. Universalization in the way Kant would want it is ethically impossible. It is in the empirical order that the mind develops principles. It is there also that principles can be tested and corrected. If our abstractions cut all links to the empirical order, they move meaninglessly away from human relevance. Purveyors of such detached abstractions will find themselves standing with Kant confessing the whereabouts of the victim to the prospective murderer — or in some equally absurd posture.

Excessive confidence in universalizability misses the complexity of principles and thus the complexity of moral life. *Ethics is a judgment of relationships in process, not of physical qualities like heat or color, and the web of relationships can never be entirely identical in all cases.*

Universalization is an unrealistic and inaccurate abstraction that passes over the fact that there are exceptions to valid moral principles. To protect other values, like the life of an intended victim, or a legitimate secret, exceptions to truth-telling must be made. Moral principles, which are grounded in the foundational moral experience and which are the voiced specifications of this experience, can and do collide with one another. Some principles by their very definition would include a set of circumstances. For example, one would be impossibly strained to find an exception to the prohibition of rape precisely because of the circumstances implied by that term. It is always amid the complexity of life and the complexity of value judgments that ethics seeks to understand the appropriate response of principles to moral value. The presupposition of ethics is that being moral means an affirmative response to value, just as being immoral means a deviant, damaging response.

Principles: Solid and Elastic...

Moral principles must be somewhat solid and somewhat elastic. They must be solid enough to preserve and make available the creative moral wisdom they encapsulate, and they must be malleable enough to yield to or be reshaped by more humanizing understandings. They vary in their elasticity or openness to exceptions. To know about principles is important for an understanding of moral discernment and ethical method generally. Principles are not all of ethics, but they are close to its center. In knowing how they operate in ethical inquiry, we will know much about how the knower knows in moral matters. For this reason, we will now look at principles from the viewpoint of moral evolution.

Principles are not the center of ethics. The discerning subject is. If the moral agent surrenders her or his unique role and reduces moral knowledge to conformism to rules, moral evolution halts. The person has defected. Principles, along with authority, group experience, and other external aids, should not do our thinking and understanding for us. The discerning moral subject is the source of creativity and is the one who has access to what is unique in the case at hand. In this sense, the morally discerning individual is the irreplaceable, immediate arbiter of what the situation means. Though it has been said that "no one is a judge in his or her own case" since one's vision may be biased by one's interests, it can, nevertheless, be said that no one else can ultimately judge the case as well as the individual involved. This individual alone has direct access to the concrete reality of the value situation. Judging alone, however, entirely apart from the social and cultural resources, is actually psychologically impossible, since we are conditioned by the environment in which we know. It would be folly not to rely consciously, but critically, on those resources. You cannot use principles as though you could inventory and catalogue the entire moral life and put its contents into definitely labeled pigeonholes, but you can be instructed by the moral experience housed in principles.

What principles properly do is supply a deeper view of the context of a case, so that the discerning subject may better discern. They cannot supply for the powers of the subject to understand the moral aspects of life. Only the subject can bring affectivity, imagination, and a dimensional sense that yield insight and understanding. If ethics were just a matter of conforming to external norms, there could be no moral growth or spontaneity. Obedience and not creativity or sensitivity would be the quintessential mark of moral persons. Ethics would be reduced to a static science of rules and applied regulations. Principles serve and illumine the discerning moral agent without displacing that person's freedom. In a legalistic structure of morality, a displacement of freedom is what happens. The result is a hardening of the moral arteries and a blocking of moral creativity and evolution. Properly used, principles can support mature and responsible change and can provide a milieu in which creativity can be distinguished from caprice.

Ethics must work on the assumption that moral maturity is attainable. At times greater protective reliance on external norms and authority figures is needed for certain individuals. Ethics should be geared to the subject who has achieved some of the autonomy that goes with psychological maturity. There are times in our moral and psychological growth when the truth of a principle comes to light only when we stand in a particular situation in which we experience the moral significance of that principle. Sometimes principles make sense to us only after we have morally grown enough to perceive their meaning.

The History and Sociology of Principles...

Principles are the moral language of social beings living in history and principles show the marks of their historical context. A highly rationalistic ethics would take little cognizance of social and historical processes and would imply that one could come upon moral principles simply by looking inward at the laws of the mind. One might indeed discover in this fashion that the whole is greater than any of its parts, but mere introspection is not the adequate source of the principles that fill our moralscape. It is important to note this point, so that there can be critical reflection regarding the principles to which we are heirs. Principles will bear the assets and the debits of social, historical existence. They must not be uncritically received because they capture the low as well as the high points of moral consciousness. It is intellectually chastening and healthy for a critical ethics to see that some principles that were long ensconced and apparently of the highest pedigree have come to be seen as wrong and immoral. The following example should temper our undue confidence in principled and established viewpoints.

Let us look to slavery, an all too recent phenomenon in American history. Slavery was surrounded and sustained by a number of well-established ethical principles that were both legally and religiously enshrined. There is grim witness here to the fact that accepted principles can be the repositories of iniquity. Holistic ethics fosters an inquisitive attitude to look into and investigate the social and historical influences of accepted moral principles. Principles are to be evaluated. Critical assessment could lead us to the refinement of principles or, in some cases, as in slavery, to radical rejection. Since moral insight is an ongoing process, ethical achievement found in principles must be affirmed continuously and, when necessary, corrected as greater moral meaning is discovered. Principles may have to be reappropriated and lost ones rediscovered.

Slavery was rationalized as being part of human nature as well as part of the nature of government. Philosophical and religious traditions supported this view. "For that some should rule and others be ruled," Aristotle says in the *Politics*, "is a thing not only necessary, but expedient; from the hour of their birth, some are marked out for subjection, others for rule." For Aristotle and for many after him, it was obviously true "that some people are by nature free, and others slaves, and that for these latter slavery is both expedient and right." Even the Bible does not condemn the institution of slavery. There is clear advice given to masters to be kind and to slaves to be obedient and these passages were often used to support the arrogance of those in power.

A number of functioning moral principles flowed from this rationalization of slavery and found expression and support in our common law. Children could be separated from parents and husbands from wives. Stanley M. Elkins in his book *Slavery* has pointed out that a North Carolina judge in 1858 wrote: "The relation between slaves is essentially different from that of man and wife joined in lawful wedlock...for with slaves it may be dissolved at the pleasure of either party, or by the sale of one or both, depending on the caprice or necessity of the owners."

Sometimes what is actually going on in culturally dominant moral principles is less apparently malignant but simply a pretentious front for what is perceived by many, and especially by those in power, as sheer necessity and moral conviction. The overused term "National Security," for example, has covered many apparent abuses of power for political expediency. The call for mandatory testing for AIDS and for drug screening can be seen as an experimentation with new principles, and those new principles are not necessarily good. In the principles that surrounded the institution of slavery, and in others, such as those supporting the subjugation of women, malignant fallacies were used to justify exploitation.

Principles, then, have the potential to be directed to ignoble or shortsighted ends, however elegantly bedecked they are with purportedly noble reasons. Principles can also become a block to moral evolution by *absolutizing* the good values that are found in them. In some ways these principles can be more dangerous than those harboring exploitative options, since they wear the credible mask of unquestioned respectability. Any right or principle that is absolutized and given an ontological, *in se* validity is in a disordered state. Rights and principles exist in relational tension with other rights and principles. Moral discernment must determine which ones, if any, apply in given situations. No principle — unless it is so generic by definition that it is more foundational than specific, such as "Do good and not evil" — should be thought to have permanent, absolute, and universal relevance.

An example of principles that have become absolutized can be those surrounding individual and property rights in America. They can easily become immune to corrective criticism and, unchallenged, they can reign as untested moral principles blinding all the ethics that is done under their unsuspected sway. But realistic ethics can help us put them into moral perspective. Property rights and individual rights are, of course, limited in the United States, as they are in any functioning nation. Taxes and the common good are obvious limits to the right of estate and the right of individual freedom. And yet there is an absolutism present in the American defense of property rights, private enterprise, and individual rights. When these rights are all operative at the same moment and in the same persons, absolutism takes on added strength. We saw these operating in their purest form in the call to shoot looters during the riots of the 1960s. In what was a sure sign of *absolutizing*, death was seen as a fitting penalty for the violation of property rights. If there is a belief in the absolute right of property, anything may go. Those who own a factory feel free to close it without giving notice to the people whose labor enriched them even though these people will be devastated by the closure. We also saw these rights working in the violent reactions to civil rights boycotts and in the foundation of private academies to exclude African Americans, a policy that amounted to using private property "rights" as a justification for violence against these Americans. The judicial system has reacted against this kind of policy, but it has its work cut out for it, since the mentality here is nourished in deep springs. Absolutized rights of freedom and ownership can render nugatory the more basic claims of persons to justice, respect, and community. The mischief is all the more difficult because it is done by people of principle and the classic conflict, in which moral evolution is resisted *on principle*, is kept going.

The upset caused by an unbalanced emphasis on certain values and certain principles is far-reaching. The American fascination with absolute liberty and with the absolute right to private property exemplifies this emphasis. The influence of the unbalance can be found in pivotal political and economic concepts such as "the national interest," "private enterprise," and "free trade." Here is where we can see the link between ethics and a science such as economics, where moral principles are also at work, as they are in all human activity. A value-conscious economics would probe deeply into its presuppositions to see what assumptions and principles it has been carrying regarding the primacy of liberty and individual ownership and to see how they affect the conclusions of economic theory and how they shape economic ideals. Economics, like any other discipline that deals with human activity, ultimately does not function without specific attitudes on what persons are and what befits them. These are foundational ethical considerations, and they should be checked.

Though economics may be defended as a legitimate and distinct discipline, it may not, like any other discipline, be presented as an ethics-free system. It is replete with estimates of what befits persons as persons — and that is the stuff of ethics. Early economists saw their work as an extension of moral philosophy, or ethics. This moral consciousness and sophistication quickly perished as economics (and the other social sciences) divorced ethics and pursued the nineteenth-century figment of a "value-free objectivity." This, of course, was nonsense, and dangerous nonsense at that. All the social sciences have built-in judgments about what persons are worth and what they deserve. Every social science is full of untested value judgments. This is belatedly and slowly being recognized as today the social sciences are starting to acknowledge that they are neck-high in moral value evaluation all the time.

Many moral principles arising out of the culture are assumed by the social sciences, given new shape and emphasis, and then returned to the culture with new force and significance. The term "value-free social science," therefore, is a crude example of false labeling. Principles do not drop down on us from the untainted realms of rarefied intellectuality. Like ourselves, they have a history. Critical ethics requires that we look to the historical and sociological roots of our principles. We cannot naively think of principles — whether they appear in ethics or in social or "hard" science — as free of historical moral conditioning.

The Rapport between Principles and Ideals...
Some principles contain practical norms, some contain ideals. Because ideals and idealists represent a call to self-criticism, they are potentially unpleasant and problematic. Idealists are discontent by nature and not well received in society. Their ideals are always pointing toward something that is not yet. But by a fortunate compensation, ideals are powerful. There has never been a major turning point in history that was not charged with idealism. All great revolutions are victories of ideals.

Although there is no perfect distinction between ideals and principles (ideals can also appear in the form of principles; "justice for all" is an example), there are distinguishing qualities. Three concentric aspects to ideals make them especially different: (1) they have a future referent, (2) they are subversive, and (3) they are gradually but never fully realized.

Some principles, such as those directing us not to kill, steal, or vandalize, are not offering ideals. They are spelling out the minimal ramifications of the foundational moral experience. Idealistic principles and ideals always promise something better. They are futuristic and based on concepts of how things might be. Second, they are subversive in the sense that they undercut the assumption that everything is as it should be. Not everything is. Because they contradict the comfortably accepted wisdom, which usually settles for less, ideals are threatening. And thirdly, ideals are gradually but never completely realized. Equality is an ideal of long standing, especially since the rise of democratic theory. Yet, there are no completely egalitarian societies. Neither are there any completely just or free societies. This does not mean that justice and freedom are mere illusions and that we abandon our quest for greater social justice. There are horizons toward which we must move, and the more we set our vision on them, the more does our moral existence reflect their light. Idealistic movements must be patient. Moral evolution may lurch forward at rare times, but in general the pace is glacierlike. Idealism can give us a hope that is not incompatible with moral growth.

The Problems of Exceptional Cases...
Principles increase our consciousness within the realm of the expectable. But moral reality has a broader reach than that. It cannot be circumscribed by principles alone nor can principles fully articulate its meaning. Also, morality involves not only rules or principles but exceptions to them. Principles are open to surprise. Sometimes principles have to be reformulated and sometimes there are unchartable situations or decisional problems that do not so much go against principles as beyond them. (Emergency situations are almost by definition beyond the

reach of facile principles.) There are moments of "ultra-obligation" and moral heroism for which there are no rules. In ethics, neither principles nor exceptions can always claim a higher status. Both are expressions of and responses to the perceived value of persons in concrete situations, and both enjoy equally sound credentials.

For a number of reasons, however, exceptions are often put on trial and argued against especially when they threaten seemingly absolute principles. Good exceptions move beyond the specific limitations of principles to a truer realization of moral value and, conversely, bad exceptions negate moral value and contradict the foundational moral experience upon which principles are based. Valid exceptions do not depart from the value housed in principles but point up their limits. The exception must be seen as a good exception to a good principle and must not threaten or diminish the value that the principle contains. Because principles cannot deal adequately with all that is unique and particular in life, exceptions are necessary. Exceptions to enduring and morally reaffirmed principles must remain exceptions and not become norms. The domino theory, which stresses that any exception to a principle will automatically lead to moral chaos, is an unrealistic way of dealing with the complexity of exceptional cases. When there seem to be more and more exceptions to a basic principle, it may mean either that the proper elasticity is being discovered in the face of mounting complexification, or it might mean that the value in the principle is receding from view. It is this latter possibility of receding value that requires a critical pause in the face of new exceptions. Exceptions, like principles, should be put on trial.

The medieval philosopher Thomas Aquinas also saw the possibility of exceptions to very basic principles so that in certain circumstances one could morally and licitly take the property of others, have sexual relations with someone other than one's spouse, and even directly kill one's self or another innocent person. He used the biblical examples of Samson committing suicide by collapsing the Philistine temple upon himself; Abraham supposedly consenting to kill his son, Isaac; and Hosea the prophet who appeared to have been implicated in sexual sin. Thomas distinguished between speculative and practical reason, the latter of which has to do with human behavior and ethics. Regarding principles of practical reason, Aquinas says: "Although there is some necessity in the common principles, the more we descend into particularities, the more frequently do we encounter defects." "Defects" here mean exceptions. The "some necessity" means that generally a moral principle will be applicable and relevant in the type of case to which it refers. The principle is good and useful but it is not absolute or not without limits, what Aquinas calls *defectus*.

There are times when a principle does not apply and under some circumstances it would be positively harmful and irrational to insist on adherence to the principle. It is a good principle to "punt on fourth down," but not when it is the end of the game and you are on the three-yard line. Exceptions occur in cases where greater values than those contained in the principle supervene and prevail. Such cases stretch across the whole gamut of human experience and ethical inquiry.

As we said earlier in chapter 6, regarding the *who?* question in the hub of the wheel model, what may be right for one person may not necessarily be right for someone else. Morality is not the same for everybody in every situation and neither are principles. If all moral meaning were absolutely generalizable, then the truth would be the same for everyone at all times. We do not want to find ourselves in the bind that Immanuel Kant was in. We do not have to tell the prospective murderer where the victim is hiding.

The truth-telling principle can run into particularities where it does not apply. In fact it would be quite moral and proper to give misleading information to the desperado. A realistic assessment of principles broadens our moral horizons and widens our response to moral value. In most cases in life, there is more than one principle making its claim to valuable relevance. There are times when principles collide and conflict with one another. Thus the ethical question here is: Which principle connects more valuably with the concrete circumstances of the case and better serves the human values at stake? One principle or the other may have to be denied temporary application. If you tell the truth, you do not save innocent life; if you save life, you do not tell the truth. Similarly, if you tell the truth, you may violate reasonable expectations of confidentiality.

No problem would exist if ethics could be reduced to the simple application of only one relevant principle to a moral situation. Neither life nor an ethics that seeks to meet its challenges is so simple. Principles cannot capture the whole of moral reality, which always contains the inimitable and the unique. There are unchartable and ungeneralizable moments. A principle is not a decision but the background to one, and, however helpful, it is inevitably limited in the face of the truly new. Moral wisdom requires that our sense of uniqueness not be dulled by the more manageable sense of what is *generally* true in principles.

12

Individual and Group Knowledge

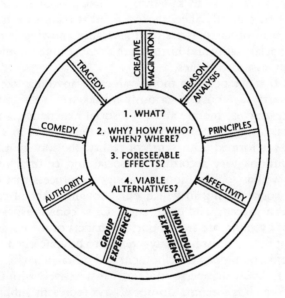

Individual and Group Experience...
We learn from personal experience as well as from the collective experience of groups. The capacity for moral discovery is as unique to the group as it is to the individual. Each has a history that offers a different emphasis on moral experience and each must be tempered by the other. In presenting *individual experience* and *group experience*, the point to be made for ethics is this: all individuals and groups are distinct sources of ethical experience, but what is unique and original in their knowing potential is not necessarily adequate. We should always systematically seek to learn from the social sources of moral insight (*group experience*) and from *individual experience*. Ethics must blend a respect for personalized original insight with a sensitivity to what is contained in the

common fund of cultural and ethical traditions. It must be critical of what is flawed in either individual or group experience and receptive of what is sound.

When we think, we always start from our social and historical matrix where interpretations of reality already exist. Even when creatively moving forward, we do not start from nowhere. The danger of not realizing our cultural and historical underpinnings is that we can lose a valuable perspective. We are born not only into the world but into a worldview in which reality, with all its specific value assumptions and positions, has been defined and assessed in certain ways. Before we are in a position to step back and gain the necessary critical distance to assess the values that we inherit from our group or society, we absorb and identify with them. If we are not aware of our social and cultural conditioning, we will be locked into it. Group influences, like peer group authority, radically affect us and for that reason we need to be aware of them in order to assess them. Because knowing is rooted de facto in our social reality and history, ethics must urge examination of unconsciously assumed values.

To think that we perceive moral values in anything like the way we see the starry sky above is seriously mistaken. To a significant extent, the "seeking" of moral values is a social experience, and even a creative moral insight is not without ties to the context in which our consciousness is formed. Our sense of reality, the way we think, and our moral outlook vary according to social and cultural influences. Knowing as well as socialization is an ongoing process that occurs in society. The social setting in which our knowing takes place gives it distinctive form, accent, and orientation. Class consciousness and nationalism, for example, are two important shapers of the human mind. One need not be a Marxist but only a realist to be concerned with class and its influence on human development and moral behavior. It would be naive not to know that persons identify instinctively with their class interests. Those class interests do not always represent sublime levels of morality or even minimal levels. Both the content and the method of our knowing are strongly conditioned by our cultural environment, and that is not a pure success story.

In considering moral issues, we need to get a critical view of the forces that are influencing us. It is chilling to think of the value judgments made by persons past and present. Although the example we now offer illustrates the negative side of group experience, it will serve the salutary purpose of demonstrating the strength that group influences have. After this illustration, we will turn to the positive uses of group experience and to the critical resource of *individual experience*.

Group experience can be ideological and can provide the basic outlook on life that is passed on through every aspect of the socialization process. Considered as the morally proper one, this outlook can explode into unimaginable frenzy that can possess the whole group and cause its members temporarily to lose their individual rationality. Group experience may even have catastrophic consequences. The witch hunts in the late seventeenth century in Massachusetts provide us with a vivid example. In her book *The Devil in Massachusetts*, Marion L. Starkey gives an excellent account of the negative effects of group experience and of how the fears of the group became a source of mass hysteria. According to Starkey the episodes in Massachusetts were not atypical happenings. Through the socialization process, the thinking, the manners, the belief, the political and religious attitudes — in a word, the whole group experience of life — foster the group's identity. Starkey mentions that the hysteria swept not only Salem but also Massachusetts Bay Colony. "The result," she says, "was by no means the most sensational example of witch hysteria on record. Only twenty witches were executed, a microscopic number compared to the tens of thousands who had been put to death in Europe and England in the course of similar outbreaks in the late Middle Ages." Group experience can be so compelling that it affects the mind and judgment of everyone. People think and act under group experience, real or imagined. The condemnation and irreversible death threats against the Anglo-Indian author Salman Rushdie are a vivid contemporary example of the negative power of group experience.

The absorbing power of our social context is a fact of cognitive life, and ethics must take it into account. Awareness is the first step toward relativizing this power and equipping us to move beyond it to greater moral sensitivity. Systematically taking account of it is part of the wholesome work of ethics and prepares the way for the creative moral mind. The cognitive influences of society must press us to ask where our minds are gripped today. In a comprehensive ethics, we should ask the question: What socially ensconced judgments are leading contemporary evaluations astray?

Many military and political experts say that only two-thirds of our military budget — or considerably less — would meet all our safety needs. Paralyzed group-think is not disposed to consider what those unneeded military expenditures could do if redirected to our needs in education, business, health care, transportation, and benign energy development. Unreflective, stubborn group-think can blind us to our own good.

On Knowing Better Socially...

Given the tendency of human beings to consume unreflectively the value positions of society, we have first pointed out the negative potential of social influence on moral evaluation. Thinking persons, however, cannot hide from society, and thought is to a substantive degree a social product. Further, we cannot think or evaluate *well* unless we deliberately appropriate the value appreciations that have arisen in our society and learn from those that have arisen in others. By recognizing that (1) thought is a social product and (2) there are value appreciations in all societies, we emphasize group experience as a positive resource in ethics. Moral knowledge and acuity profit from the trusting appropriation of the wisdom and experience of our own society *and* from comparisons and contrasts with diverse social experiences. We gain an invaluable perspective from other groups and societies.

It should be obvious that, to a substantial degree, our society shapes us. What this fact uncovers is our finitude and the humanizing exigency of trust. The moral universe is comparable to the physical universe in scope and mystery. No single person can explore it. Even together, our reach is limited. So, naturally and inevitably, we tune in to the knowing processes of others. By necessity, knowing is a shared process. But ethics is not merely charting the necessities but also speaking normatively of what ought to be done. Communal appreciations should be tapped, whether they exist in the present or whether they can be partially retrieved from history. Here group experience relates to what was said about the spoke on authority. Complementarity and reliance are integral to our social being. Trust is an essential ingredient in the process of becoming *more* human. This trusting pattern is a noble trait of human life. It enters into evaluations and conjoins us to the moral achievements of humankind. The example of the Salem witch trial, an event that illustrates the possibility of mindless absorption into group consciousness, was not intended to supplant trust. Rather, it was used to urge that our trust retain a critical edge, without which it would deteriorate into blind emotion.

Related here, too, is our treatment of principles, since it is through principles that group consciousness and moral sensitivity are significantly articulated. In critically appropriating principles and other moral practices of our society, we are acknowledging that that society, even for all its moral failures, has not been entirely unmoved before the mysterious values of personhood. The comparing of diverse group and societal experiences can help balance one's own cultural value appropriations.

At the present time in the United States, there is a keen interest in studying Japan. The extraordinary economic success of the Japanese signals some better ways of doing things. Some of what is found in Japan is not imitable. Other things, such as attention to job security, better rapport between labor and management, tapping the labor force for ideas, and so forth, contain both business and ethical lessons that may be imitable. Active, intelligent concern for the needs of persons in the work force is conducive to greater productivity. It is another example of *good ethics* as *good business.*

Making sense of things is the passion of the mind. Sometimes when we have had some sense-making success, we tend to freeze our insight, forgetting that it is only partial and forgetting too that truth for us is a process of attunement and never a completed product. Cultural absolutism is the blight of sensitive moral intelligence. This freezing into absolutes happens in all fields of thought. The central moral faculty of creative imagination is regularly blocked in every intellectual discipline and in every culture by the difficulty of penetrating unchallenged, long-tenured orthodoxies. Sensitivity to what other groups think or have thought on matters that concern us can be effective solvents of false absolutes. Rather than simply being immersed only in the particular ethical issues that emerge in our society, ethics should press us to look at different kinds of moral presuppositions that emerge in other social systems. The reason is that if you do not check your presuppositions, you may, for example, end up spelling out with punctilious ingenuity the rights and duties that slaves have instead of questioning the institution of slavery itself. Drawing other group and social experiences into view can yield valuable perspective, positive or negative. Some group experiences may affirm or correct our value positions; others, through detailed analysis and comparison, may need to be rejected as morally unfit. But in both cases, group experience is a critical resource that is meant to expand our moral awareness.

For example, how is it that our health care system is beset with some forty million uninsured people? How have other nations avoided this tragic shortfall? The problem here is moral, not material, since we may be the richest nation in the world in material resources. If poorer nations have ways of bringing health care to all their citizens, we should, in this regard, be their ethics students.

In the absence of all contrast, questions about our social and moral conditioning could remain unasked, leaving us incapable of moral criticism. The discovery of such question-breeding social and group contrasts is a necessary task of ethics. In reference to diverse societies and groups, anthropology and sociology have done a major service to ethics by discovering the wide variety within human mores, thus providing us with many contrasts. The experience of variety pushes us to look to the roots of our own standards as a way of moving more deeply into moral truth. In ethics, as in art, contrast heightens perception by giving a different and fuller perspective. Consciousness of diverse group experience in any area of morality can liberate us from the constricting grip of our own biases or can reaffirm the soundness of our own experiences. But fixated attention on only one other historical experience can easily be a block to moral discourse. (See chapter 16, where we discuss the notion of false analogies.) Like the differences concerning the *who?* question in the hub of the wheel model, what might be morally defensible for one group or society may not necessarily be morally defensible for another. There is a difference between knowing and knowing more fully. Ethically, to know more fully is to be aware of diverse group experience.

The Pendulum Effect...
We should also take account of the pendulum effect in the history of human thought when discussing group consciousness and diverse group experience. The pendulum is a fitting symbol for human knowing. Knowledge develops in a field of action and reaction. In reaction against certain errors, the pendulum shifts and can easily swing too far in the opposite direction. We can go from Victorian prudishness on sex to unrestrained pornography, from undertreating to overtreating in medicine, from ignoring AIDS to insensitive mandatory testing, and from regulation to deregulation and back again in the world of business. To and fro is the way of human thought and evaluation.

Trust in the established mores and authorities in society can yield to *asocial* conceptions of freedom and glorification of doing one's own thing. Confidence in the general principles and reliance on that which is commonly true can produce a counterreaction in which only the unique and unrepeatable is championed. Depending on where the pendulum is, rules and exceptions may be on trial. The pendulum can move from one extreme to the other or veer off to new extremes and overreact against overreaction. The pendulum swing can exercise a conservative role of recovery and, if it does not overlook the values in that which it reacts against, its service for group consciousness can be considerable.

Developing an acute sense of the pendular movements of thought is essential to critical judgment. Critical thinkers must always check to see where the pendulum is carrying them with forces that they did not create. Ethics should act as a weight on the pendulum, to keep it from flying off too far in extreme reaction and overreaction. What is needed is a discipline of the mind whereby we force ourselves to consider the values in that which we are reacting against.

The following could be taken as a working rule, not as an absolute principle but as a guiding assumption: *If anything has been held by a large number of persons for a long period, it most likely is not completely valueless.* It may in the main be erroneous and in need of drastic criticism. However, if we may assume that pure error is unimaginable, there is probably something worthy of retrieval even in highly erroneous group positions. In criticizing or rejecting an extreme, ethics must look for hidden values and make distinctions between them and the accompanying disvalues that need correction.

The pendulum can swing away from many positions and into new and uncharted areas. Today we can see the pendulum swinging into such areas as genetic engineering, selective abortion or pregnancy reduction of multiple fetuses, surrogate mothering, mandatory drug testing, and psychological screening of job applicants. New technologies offer new freedoms that easily push the pendulum away from former positions. The question for ethics is whether a particular pendulum movement is good or bad.

In Defense of the Living Intellect: Individual Experience...

"An ethical system," John Henry Newman wrote in *A Grammar of Assent*, "may supply laws, general rules, guiding principles, a number of examples, suggestions, landmarks, limitations, cautions, distinctions, solutions of critical or anxious difficulties; but who is to apply them to a particular case? Whither can we go, except to the living intellect, our own, or another's?" Individual experience and personal responsibility are of great importance in ethical decision-making. "The authoritative oracle, which is to decide our path," Newman continues, "...is seated in the mind of the individual, who is thus his own law, his own teacher, and his own judge in those special cases of duty which are personal to him."

Newman's words introduce our consideration of the unique credentials of the individual discerning subject. This spoke on *individual experience* overlaps with others in our holistic model of ethical method. That there is shared ground here and elsewhere is not only recognized and admitted but necessary for a complete ethical system that attempts to be critically comprehensive of moral circumstances. In treating creative imagination, affectivity, and authority, for example, the special prerogatives of the individual's knowing capacity have been acknowledged. For this reason, we may treat this particular spoke more concisely. Special status is given to individual experience in order to supply an emphasis that should be corrective of a common distortion. Trust in one's own unique powers of moral knowing is not commonplace. Much of our moral stability is found by clinging to others, and in doing so we end up relying on — and perhaps absolutizing — group experience. Could we not rely more on our own individual experience especially when in our hearts and consciences we may know something to be morally defensible? To work from the original center of our own experiences may be exceptional but it is not impossible. Creative moral leaders who have turned us inside out with their moral vision exemplify the originality and confidence in the experience of the self. Even in less extraordinary and history-turning ways, we all know some persons who exhibit a freshness in their value consciousness that comes from their ability to be something other than faithful mirrors. Still, let us grant the rarity of the purely original mind.

Given our social nature, originality is more a matter of degree. But some minds are almost completely strapped to their social props, and others, less so. This is a point that must be of interest to ethics. Ethics seeks to point the way to value awareness that is fully alive. If persons choke on their own unique perceptive powers and timidly repair to crowd-think, the community of valuing animals is to some degree crippled. Such huddled thinking must yield something of a blur. To hang together it must rely heavily on stereotypes and generalizations. To preserve itself, crowd-think must shy away from the singularity that can be discerned by "the living intellect."

Two things must be kept in mind in championing the prestige of individual cognitive experience: the first is the uniqueness of the individual and the second is the uniqueness of every situation. It is no poetic license to say that each human being is distinct and unrepeatable. Even physiologically the very structure of our bodies and our brains suggests this uniqueness. Psychologically, too, we are all different and do not fall into exactly the same patterns. Furthermore, no two persons have identical experiences or histories. Nor do any two persons react to the same reality in an identical way. Since affectivity is one of the ways in which we are morally aware, another variable source of uniqueness presents itself.

Moral insight gives a view of reality refracted through the personal experience of a unique cognitive structure. In the conscious awareness that we call knowledge, a vital and multidimensional process of attunement, interpretation, filtering, accenting, and imagining is going on. The process reflects the complex singularity of the knower and this reflection is especially true in the knowledge of values. It has been said that any work of art is reality refracted through a temperament. Any moral judgment is similarly personalized.

Individual experience can actually affirm some group experience because the personal nuances, although different for each individual, do not differ so radically that one's moral decision is by necessity different from another's. Individual experience may authenticate or rediscover a lost moral insight of other individuals and of groups, further verifying the growth of the foundational response to moral value.

Attention has to be drawn to the knowledge gained from personal experience because confidence in our own perceptive powers is slight. We fly to that which is similar, unsure of that which is different in us. We fear our own creativity. Socially endorsed positions seem more reliable. One result of this reliability can cause us to lose confidence in our own "common sense." It is a sad fact of intellectual life that persons will sacrifice their best insights to the accepted opinions of the group. But we, individually, are the valuing and deciding animal and we shrink from our responsibilities as moral human beings when we place excessive reliance on social sources of insight. There should be a balance between *group* and *individual experience*, each adding moral insight to the other.

Like persons, situations are unique and in a state of flux. Ethics swims in crosscurrents, where new patterns and new problems are always emerging. The established wisdom, drawn from past experiences, may not be enough for judging that which is new. The burden falls on "the living intellect" of the individual. But the responsibility for individual assessment does not extend just to concrete behavioral decisions. It also imposes the burden of evaluating the values that we have inherited from our society, as far as that is possible. We are not destined to be controlled by crowd-think in the same way that lesser animals are controlled by instinct, though it would appear that crowd-think is our substitute for the instinctive apparatus that we would prefer to moral responsibility. There is an irremediable loneliness to moral knowledge and to individual moral decision-making. We are never wholly melted into an unindividuated group consciousness. Group experience should deepen and consolidate our individuality and should not blot out our unique cognitive resources. It is to this end that *individual experience* as an evaluational spoke is directed.

Religious Experience...

Religion is an important bearer of moral attitudes and judgments. Its moral content relates to both individual and group experience. The literature of the major religions, represented in contemporary societies, abounds in moral teaching. Sometimes this teaching is in very specific terms that easily become dated and encrusted in a contextually insensitive code of conduct. However, religious experience has historically served the "valuing animal" in such wise that theoreticians of ethics ignore it to their own impoverishment. Unfortunately, some philosophical ethicists of our day are inclined to overlook or disregard the moral content and ethical service of religious traditions. Feeling that these sources are tainted with sectarian bias, they, perhaps, believe that religious insights concerning moral value are unreliable and unworthy of the philosophical enterprise. Their attitude is intellectually limited and, from the view of ethical method, unsound. Their enterprise is directed to the critical uncovering of truth, which includes moral truth. Good ethical method is sensitive to all the sources of moral valuation, whether those sources are religiously or nonreligiously affiliated. Good ideas do not need special passports to enter an open mind.

There are two principal ways in which moral insight derives from major religious traditions. First, these traditions significantly affirm the validity and prerogatives of individual experience in valuation. Alfred North Whitehead points this out in his study *Religion in the Making:* "The moment of religious consciousness starts from self-valuation, but it broadens into the concept of the world as a realm of adjusted values, mutually intensifying or mutually destructive." One can be eclectic in learning value insights from the religious traditions. There is no long-tenured tradition, religious, political, or other, that is not encumbered with unhappy and even absurd accretions. We can learn from these traditions without becoming tied to their errors. Second, religions are major vehicles of group experience containing as they do a good deal of the moral appreciations and discoveries of groups. The great religions constitute a particular vision or, rather, a number of harmonized (or partly harmonized) visions of what the shape of the moral life is.

The notion of God, in fact, often recapitulates in a poetic way the basic notions of what moral goodness entails, as perceived by a particular people. Each religious tradition was forged on the anvil of an unrepeatable time in history, marked by special challenges. Its moral vision and interpretations will be distinguished by its presuppositions, collective attitudes, geography, history, mood, myths, analogues, symbols, and saints. Different things will be cared about, and, again, caring is intrinsic to knowing. The result is that each religious tradition should be looked to as a unique locus of moral interpretation, where distinctive perceptions of what does or does not befit the mysterious phenomenon of personhood have been achieved. Irrelevancies are also to be anticipated, reflecting the unique aspects of the original experience. But valid insights may also be awaited, wrought from the experiences of a reflective people and enshrined in the literary and oral traditions of that people.

There are certain inevitable dialectical tensions that present themselves to moral understanding. We must all somehow take our stand on the conflicting claims of pessimism and hope, of the individual and the common good, of creativity and conformism, of authority and initiative, of ecstasy and order. We must fashion or assume a conception of what power, justice, and love imply. The various religious traditions have responded to these points in ways that have *potentially* universal benefit. Each of us, like the travellers in Geoffrey Chaucer's *Canterbury Tales*, has a story to tell, and it is our business to know our story. Because of our story, we can teach what others do not know, and then we can listen to learn something of what we have missed that others have found. This openness can also be commended regarding the various philosophical traditions, but we here stress the religious sources of moral wisdom, since they are so regularly neglected in the ethical treatment of group experience in our secular age.

13

The Comic and the Tragic
in Ethics

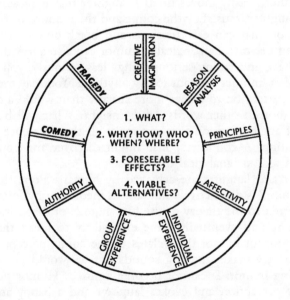

The Moral Value of Humor and Suffering...

The last two critical resources represented by the spokes of the wheel model relate to the tragic and comic realities of life and to how they affect moral evaluation. *Tragedy* and *comedy* are more closely allied than most people think and together they offer valuable interpretations of human behavior. They contain direct revelations filled with ethical meaning. First, we will turn to the comic mode of moral insight and then to the tragic.

The history of ethics shows that humor (a term that we are using interchangeably with comedy) has not been given a prominent place in the systematic study of morality. It is not that comedy has been ignored by all philosophers. The bibliography of J. Y. Greig's *Psychology of Laughter and Comedy* mentions 363 works devoted wholly or partially to the subject. The authors range from Plato and Aristotle to Kant, Bergson, and Freud. Still, the interest in humor has not led to its inclusion as an integral part of ethical method. This absence indicates a serious omission. There are many modes of moral consciousness and one of them is humor. Humor has the delightful talent of being able to penetrate issues in nonthreatening ways. By briefly explaining what humor is and what it achieves, we can show its significant role as an evaluational resource.

Humor, among other things, involves a creative response to incongruity and surprise. As a way of seeing and relating to things, it provides insight and implies a sympathetic understanding of human nature. Humor easily moves us to a laughter that is pleasant and engaging. Laughter, caused by the comic and the humorous, is a relaxing phenomenon that can ease tensions and break down artificial barriers between persons. Paradoxically, humor can also allow distance. By stepping back and taking serious things less seriously, you can laugh at yourself or another without losing anything. You may even succeed in drawing attention to things more sharply than would a dour judgment. Humor, in other words, lends insight. What will be gained is a different angle of vision that can make all the difference in human understanding. A comic response might discover and communicate more than tedious analytical discourses.

Humor and laughter are achieved by humans alone. In fact, the word "humor" is distinctively human. In medieval physiology, it originally referred to the theory of the four liquids or dispositions of the human body and eventually came exclusively to mean that particular disposition or humor that relates to the comic perception of life. The hyena may make laughing sounds but we would not say that it is displaying humor. It cannot become amused. Humor presupposes intelligent perception and evokes laughter and a happy amusement. Whatever it is that humor has that causes laughter is debatable, but most theories agree that laughter is provoked by some incongruity or inconsistency. Humor, from childish jokes to sophisticated witticisms, lives on surprise and discrepancy. Humor involves an intellectual reaction and represents an appraisal of incongruities within human experience.

The fact that we are the unique subjects and objects of laughter should have sent initial signals to ethics. We laugh at what is human and human-like. Ethics is concerned with the human. It should, therefore, be fully alert to any reaction that is wholly centered on humanness. This fact alone raises intriguing suspicions of relevance. No specific intellectual and affective manifestation (such as humor and laughter) should be ignored by the art/science that seeks to understand and evaluate the whole phenomenon of humanness.

Along with incongruity, humor involves surprise or the unexpected. It can give a *new* twist to something that is familiar. The surprise element is visible all the way from the peekaboo laughter of the baby to the comments of an accomplished satirist. A good example of the moral edge in humor can be found in a remark by Mark Twain: "It is by the goodness of God that in our country we have those three unspeakably precious things: freedom of speech, freedom of conscience, and the prudence never to practice either of them." The initial piety of the comment sets us up for the surprising ending. The humor comes from the inconsistency between the professed love of freedom and the fear of using it. The incongruity and the unexpected factors are of the essence of humor. The repeated joke fails and the joke that has to be explained takes away the surprising newness.

Humor is also a work of creativity and, as such, it includes a sensitivity to proper timing (*kairos*). The creative mind perceives connections and similarities that are missed in the more literal and blunt views of the facts of life, and it knows how and when to express that perception. Because of creative achievement, the humorist gives us more than a good laugh. We achieve a better understanding of reality. The following passage, found in *Literary History of the United States*, speaks directly to our concerns here: "More effectively even than folklore — from which it has persistently borrowed — American humor from colonial days to the present has acted as a catalytic agent for the changes in our expanding nation and its mingled peoples." Our growth as a nation, like that of any nation, has been awkward and uneven and humor has always been there too in its unique role.

There is creative imagination behind humor and further serious reflection of an enlightening nature might take place because of it. Humor is more than just one of the respectable and normal avenues for the growth of moral awareness. It may at times be the only avenue open to moral insight and imagination. To bypass the use of this resource, because it does not suit our pompous rationalistic conceptions of how proper ethics should be done, is unintelligent. There may be no setting where humor is out of place.

The comic insight expresses a definite attitude toward life. It is a celebration of values that arouse an awareness of human possibilities. Humor is necessary moral equipment. It adds a different and often needed tone to reality. It is a positive experience that offers a possible way of resolving conflict as well as being one that engenders hope and healing. Norman Cousins, in his book *Anatomy of an Illness*, gives vivid and convincing evidence of the therapeutic role of humor and laughter. "I made the joyous discovery," he writes, "that ten minutes of genuine belly laughter had an anesthetic effect and would give me at least two hours of pain-free sleep.... I was greatly elated by the discovery that there is a physiologic basis for the ancient theory that laughter is good medicine." The comic response to life is an affirmative resource and ought not be a forgotten aspect of ethics.

Humor can be a manifestation of a hope that is potentially recreative and never destructive. Derisory and perverted humor, of course, can represent despair because its purpose is vindictive. Humor and laughter are among the appropriate responses to reality, and that has to be reassuring because it suggests that tragedy does not have the final and only word. Hope perdures in humor, a fact that is at once delightful and relevant to ethics.

There is some truth in the saying that life is a tragedy for those who think and a comedy for those who feel. There is also some error in it, since tragedy and comedy can no more be separated than can thought and feeling. The truth of the saying, however, is in the linkage of humor and feeling. Humor is as much an affective response to value as it is an intellectual one and it is as much a conduit of moral truth as character and feelings are. Comedy embodies a hopeful judgment about life.

To assist further in showing how the spoke comedy is germane to ethical evaluation, we can look to one of the problems confronting critical thinking, the problem of false absolutes. A major goal in ethics is to counter this problem, and humor is an important force in achieving this goal. Humor serves a relativizing function in the face of apparent absolutisms such as, for example, rationalism and power. A humorous mindset comports a habit of anticipating newness and surprise. In a mind where it is at home there will be less rigidity and more suppleness of spirit, qualities that well befit a "living intellect."

Humor thrives on paradox and on the recognition that there are times when we simply cannot "get it together," when we are left with the likeness of truth on both horns of an intellectual dilemma. Rationalism wants to explain everything. Humor knows that that cannot be done and that there is understanding that surpasses rational explanation. Humor is a healthy reminder of how variegated and ultimately mysterious understanding is. It is thus a force for modesty and intellectual realism. It does not fight rationalism by going against reason but by enlightening it. Humor is not antirational. It presents another way of viewing the same facts; thus humor is a native and primordial source for the expansion of the mind.

Humor can play an active role in adding a needed dimension to positions of power. When power is absolutized and cut off from the essential human task of building community among persons, it can easily corrupt those in positions of authority. Political and social cartoonists, for example, relativize power by putting it into a comic perspective that illuminates its limits. The power that operates among persons must be intertwined with other human values and never become an end in itself. Power and authority are to remain means validated and balanced by their service to human ends. The comic influence should be present in such centers as Congress, the White House, the Kremlin, and the Board Room. The medievals were wise when they insistently installed the jester in all the halls of power. The lord, the prince, and the bishop were all the institutionalized prey of the jester's taming wit. There is a place for humor in every professional setting. Indeed, a sense of humor is a prerequisite for anyone in a position of leadership and authority.

When Humor Goes Amuck...

An ancient saying tells us: "The corruption of that which is best, is the worst" (*Corruptio optimi pessima*). Humor is among the best of our human characteristics. Thus the ways in which it can go awry must not be missed. For one thing, strained humor might be a work of despair and resignation. We ought not laugh when we should weep or when we should be indignant. Such humor trivializes human value.

Further, laughter can be an expression of ridicule or derision, but that laughter is contemptuous and closer to hostility than humor. It is the laughter of Iago in Shakespeare's *Othello*. Many of our skewed valuations are driven into us by derision and ridicule. There are negative, as well as positive, social forces at work in the way we learn to perceive others. Sexism and racism, for example, are re-enforced through a demeaning humor and deviations from such attitudes are often mocked and ridiculed. Sometimes laughter is not always in keeping with moral value. Derisive humor used by those in authority can be cruel and counterproductive. But there are kinds of humor where the humorous spirit plays on the border line not only between jest and earnest but also between comedy and tragedy without belittling people.

The Positive Value of Tragedy...

We have listed tragedy as one of the spokes of the ethical wheel model because it has a potentially positive value for the expansion of moral consciousness. Each spoke represents a personal or cultural resource through which moral understanding is advanced.

It may seem impossible to speak in praise of suffering without lapsing into sadism or masochism. Yet we know that suffering seems intrinsic to living. It also seems to be a crucible from which significant experiences can influence the growth of moral consciousness. We are not suggesting that we ought not try to do away with suffering. Medical science, for example, has eliminated many forms of suffering and tragedies from life. This fact is an obvious good. Whenever we can, it is our moral duty to contain and prevent tragedy. Suffering has no intrinsic value.

Whether suffering contributes positively to our moral growth depends entirely on our response to it. What is special about persons is their ability to transcend suffering and to transform it into something good. Tragedy can expand moral awareness by giving us greater moral sensitivity. To any discernible degree, other animals do not have this capacity. A horse, for instance, that becomes deaf and blind early in its life would be best put to death. Helen Keller, however, had these disabilities and yet she was able to transcend them and bring fulfillment to herself and hope to others. Her greatness related to her tragedy. There is moral growth in Helen Keller's response to this suffering. It sharpens appreciation of our human capacities of caring and loving. Our consciousness is drawn more deeply into the foundational moral experience of the value of persons.

One way of sensing the potential value of tragedy is to consult our own experience of the positive things it can do to people. H. Richard Niebuhr addresses this point in his book *The Responsible Self*, where he says that "everyone with any experience of life is aware of the extent to which the characters of people he has known have been given their particular forms by the sufferings through which they have passed." Niebuhr insists that what changes people is due more to how they respond to what happens than to the event that occurs. He asserts that "it is in the response to suffering that many and perhaps all [people], individually and in their groups, define themselves, take on character, develop their ethos." It would seem to be within the experience of all of us that deep suffering can bring greater depth and sensitivity to persons who were, before that, overly self-assured and superficial. It is also true, of course, that suffering can break a person, and this too is revealed by even a little of life's experience.

What is being said here in terms of ethical method is that our response to suffering can bring moral depth to our character and can make our affective response to moral truth more sensitive. As we discussed in reference to the spoke *affectivity*, it is within character that the truth of moral experience resonates. The affective and characterological orientation wrought by well-met tragedy provides a deeper compassion, an essential component of moral knowing. The character of individuals and of groups or of whole nations can be fashioned not so much by the professed ideals of these individuals or groups, as by the way they meet situations in which suffering cannot be avoided. To know how a person or a society has responded to suffering is to know much of the good or the bad of that person, of that society. This knowledge also helps in analyzing the individual and group experiences that must be consulted in a moral method. In a hospital setting, patients (the

THE COMIC AND THE TRAGIC IN ETHICS

word comes from the Latin meaning "one who suffers") have a lot to teach the hospital staff about humane medicine. Their suffering gives them a podium from which to speak. Attention to the tragic elements in individual and group histories is important and the question must be asked whether the suffering has embittered or ennobled the sufferer. These are important reasons why tragedy can be listed as one of the spokes of ethical method.

How Can the Tragic Be Good?

Some suggestion can be made about how our response to suffering may have a positive effect on our moral character and consciousness. In speaking of tragedy or suffering, we refer to a painful experience that is not of our own choosing, one that thwarts our plans and hopes, and one that we would avoid if at all possible. What good, then, could such a thing as suffering possibly do? *And*, why would we look to tragedy for positive contributions?

To understand something of how suffering can be beneficial to moral growth, it is well to know what suffering is not. First, suffering is not unhappiness any more than pleasure is happiness. Suffering, of course, can lead to unhappiness and depression, in which event it submerges the powers of the person and crushes the mind and spirit. Here, suffering becomes overwhelming and absolute. If there is meaning that endures in spite of the suffering, then the tragic dimension will not blot out hope or stifle the processes of moral growth. If tragedy produces only unhappiness, we could expect the gradual extinction of the personal powers of the sufferer. Second, the positive evaluation of suffering is not a collapse into masochism. Ethical method takes a positive view of tragedy because persons can and may become more compassionate and humane in response to suffering. Personal and cognitive growth might occur during the suffering and because of it. The value is in the sufferer and not in the suffering itself. Masochism, on the contrary, involves a perverted and debasing glorification of pain. The possibility of persons to advance during the worst of times and to bring value from the apparently valueless gives tragedy the potential to offer a positive perspective in moral evaluation.

Tragedy intensifies awareness of reality as process and ultimately as unpredictable. It can also strike directly at a moral blind spot where one does not perceive value until suffering occurs. Tragedy shakes the foundations of the mind and can produce a more humble attitude. Nothing is quite the same after a tragedy. It cannot but touch our complacent and misguided patterns of interpretation because it always involves a shocking recognition of how terrible something can be. Tragedy stuns our smugness. It is a powerful reminder that not all is as we imagine or expect. Even if we, to some degree, were to anticipate a tragedy, we would still be shocked by it. Tragedy is not experienced by anticipation.

Because in tragedy we learn that life can produce the shock of pain and suffering, we are less disposed to circumscribe reality or to trust our conceptions of what reality truly is. The tragic experience introduces new horizons as it forces itself into the center of our conscious existence. It brings us into contact with struggles that confront the full measure of our humanity. The change in consciousness, however, that follows tragedy is not necessarily for the better. One's view can be distorted by pain and an opportunity for growth can be missed. But tragedy, if borne well, can open moral perspective in ways that would otherwise be impossible.

Again, to apply this to the world of medicine, nurses and doctors who have had intimate professional contact with various forms of suffering have done a kind of ethics that should be fed into hospital policies. The patients, or the parents of patients, who have had the tragic experience of some illness, are indispensable witnesses for the ethics of caring for victims of that disease. The same is true for other fields. What journalist would be considered mature and seasoned who had not weathered tough times and learned from the experience? Though we sensibly would like to avoid it when possible, it remains a stubborn fact of life that some learning occurs only in challenging and suffering situations. Those who suffer through the agonies of business, medicine, and politics should have special insights, but, of course, they may also have their blind spots.

Tragedy in Relation to Other Spokes...
The spoke on tragedy relates especially to two other spokes on the wheel model, *affectivity* and *creative imagination*. Tragedy can spark challenge and challenge can stimulate our responsive feelings and creativity. It also summons courage. "Fear has large eyes," says a Russian proverb. It sees with painful keenness all that is a threat. But courage has larger eyes. It sees beyond the circumstances of distress and suffering and reaches for the possibilities that the fearful do not perceive. The courageous mind can be affective and creative. Courage represents a flourishing of the human spirit and a morally commanding response of persons beset by tragic experience. Suffering calls forth affective sensitivity and creative response. Anyone who loves and attempts great things will not be unacquainted with suffering. Love extends our vulnerability and expands the area in which we face and feel risk. The persecution of excellence, in particular, of moral excellence, is a prominent, persistent, and sad theme in human history. If someone would move sensitively and creatively, i.e., morally, in society to work for justice and criticize injustice, tragedy and suffering are to be expected.

Society does not readily entertain challenges to low standards of justice and fairness.

In Conclusion...
We have completed our discussion of the nine spokes of the wheel model regarding ethical method. Through these evaluational resources our consciousness is enhanced when facing moral issues. It should be clear that the several spokes are diverse in nature. In assessing a particular problem, it is not possible to sit down and summon these evaluational elements as one might call in a group of witnesses, each in an assigned turn. Some of these spokes may have limited use in certain morally adjudicable cases. There are, for example, heroic situations that call for unique and instant solutions for which no principles can adequately prescribe. Sometimes when principles seem to collide irreconcilably, we are cast more upon affective appreciations. Similarly, there are situations of impasse where old solutions clearly will not do and creative imagination must strain to find the answer.

There is, of course, no implication here that when persons are faced with a sudden moral decision they will withdraw, sketch out the wheel model of ethics, and plod from point to point. Such immediate decisions are made by conscience, by the morally conscious self attuned to values as they emerge in the concrete situation. The reaction of conscience is often "on the spot" when there may be virtually no time for reflection. The nature of conscience will be discussed in the next chapter, but here it is mentioned to note its distinction from detached ethical reflection. Reflection always requires time, whereas conscience must normally respond to the urgency of action. Conscience, however, is always nourished in reflection, and ethics, as a reflective way of knowing moral value, is one of its sources.

Still, it is possible to press the mind in a fairly systematic way to turn to seven of the evaluational modes that we discussed. We can insist upon attention to the potential contribution of *creative imagination, affectivity, reason and analysis, authority, principles, individual* and *group experience*. We can check for neglect in each of these areas and seek to avoid the pitfalls of a one-sided approach. We cannot in an equally systematic way invoke the *tragic* and the *comic* perception while assessing a particular case of moral concern. Awareness of the positive aspects of comedy and tragedy in one's worldview, however, can introduce perspective. They are potential avenues of moral insight. A sense of the significance of the comic and tragic views can function influentially at the level of presupposition. Openness to their evaluative role can create a mental climate that leaves us less likely prey to an incompleteness that deters the processes of knowing. Awareness of all the ways in which we know is the essence of moral sophistication.

It should also be noted that one's method may not be explicit in all cases of ethical analysis. Method is not technique or tactic. The delineation of a method is a way of charting out with self-conscious modesty the manifold aspects of the phenomenon of knowing. Following the method suggested here does not mean that when we study some moral problem we always need to have bobbing at the surface every one of its explicitated elements. The validity of this method should be detectably implicit in all our particular analyses of normative issues. We should always "do ethics" with alertness to the various ways in which moral truth is attained. One need not stop and say: "See, I have not forgotten spoke number four in my discussion of this or that issue." But when the discussion is completed, it should not show neglect of what the spokes represent in our knowing potential.

We will turn next to a discussion of the very important notion of *conscience* and to its role in moral judgments.

STUDY QUESTIONS

Re: The Evaluational Phase

1. Explain the purpose of the evaluational phase of ethical method and how it relates to the reality-revealing questions. Are the spokes always to be trusted? Show how each spoke could betray or assist you in making moral decisions.

Re: Creative Imagination

2. Discuss the growth of moral imagination and the conditions for moral creativity. Pick one professional setting and show how the conditions for moral creativity would transform and improve the situation.

3. How does creative imagination relate to viable alternatives? How would you creatively structure an international "strike force" to react to oil spills anywhere on earth within a short period?

4. Creative ways are needed to solve many of our problems. How would you best analyze the options for waste disposal? The industrialized nations are now attempting to "dump" their wastes on third world nations. Discuss the problem of corporations exporting jobs to third world nations because of the extremely low wage schedules there. What moral and creative options do these corporations have? Comment.

5. How do creative movements spawn other creative movements? Give some examples. Why are creative people often persecuted?

Re: Affectivity

6. Is there a link between affectivity and creativity? Between affectivity and reason? Explain.

7. How do feelings enter into moral evaluation right from the start? In what ways do feelings bring insight? Can one's affective response to a moral issue be wrong? Explain. Give some examples of how your feelings have been right, have been wrong.

8. To what extent is character part of our own choosing? Is a person's moral character due more to nature, nurture, or choice?

9. Give some examples of how modern life has given us a greater need for acknowledging affectivity and its legitimate role? Explain. Is affectivity more stunted in men than in women? Do men and women tend to have the same approach to moral value questions? Give examples from your own experience.

Re: Reason and Analysis

10. Can reason ever be "purified" of all prejudice and self-interest? Explain.

11. Explain the expression: "Fortune favors the prepared mind."

Re: Authority

12. Why does authority have such an influence on moral thinking and decision making? How free can you be or should you be from authorities?

13. "Religion" refers to a sense of the sacred. Explain how nationalism and patriotism are imbued with *religious* authority.

Re: Principles

14. Moral principles have residual effects. They can live on through our institutions and attitudes. Discuss some of the residual effects of the principles that supported certain forms of behavior that we as a nation have now come to reject, behavior such as slavery and the denial of voting rights for women.

15. How can good principles have exceptions? How valid is the domino theory, that one exception leads to another and so on until exceptions become the norm? Give an evaluation. Is the moral truth of a principle relevant for everybody in every situation? Can principles collide with one another? Should a nurse or physician or journalist always tell the truth, the whole truth, and nothing but the truth? Are there no exceptions to this principle? Does a businessperson have an obligation to tell everything about a product?

16. Discuss, evaluate, and give some examples of the following statement: The truth of a principle may come to light only when one is ready for it, when one has acquired the experiential and moral maturity to understand it. Might you not understand some values and principles as a parent that you did not see clearly prior to the experience of parenthood?

Re: Individual and Group Experience

17. Discuss the powers and perils of peer authority. What happens if you accept peer authority too much, too little?

18. Give some examples of how group experience can correct individual experience and of how individual experience can correct group thinking on moral issues.

19. Give examples of how we often seem to rely on group experience even when we may know in our hearts that our own experience is morally defensible?

20. Show how small group experience can enlighten the minds of individuals and of society. Explain how small groups, like the handicapped, can instruct the larger society. Can you think of other examples?

Re: Comedy and Tragedy

21. Clarify the terms "comedy" and "tragedy." In what ways can comedy and tragedy promote a fuller sense of the moral and the human? Comedy and tragedy seem like opposites, but what similar results do they have?

22. Show how humor can relativize and lend insight into human situations. Give examples.

PART FOUR

Conscience and
the Moral Self

14

Conscience

"Conscience" is a term that suffers from overfamiliarity, and yet it is difficult to define. The Oxford English Dictionary tells us that "opinions as to the nature, function, and authority of conscience are widely divergent, varying from the conception of the mere exercise of the ordinary judgment on moral questions, to that of an infallible guide of conduct, a sort of deity within us."

Hamlet saw conscience as a restraint against wrongdoing; Milton saw it as an "umpire"; Aquinas as "the pedagogue of the soul"; Locke as simply our own opinion in moral matters; and Byron called it "the oracle of God." Some reduce conscience to the Freudian "superego" or to a mere echo of the social mores. Many people agree with the eighteenth-century philosopher Joseph Butler, who said that "we have a capacity of reflecting upon actions and characters, and making them an object to our thought; and on doing this, we naturally and unavoidably approve some actions, under the peculiar view of their being virtuous and of good desert; and disapprove others, as vicious and of ill desert." Some take this statement to mean that we have within us an innate moral sense to achieve instant ethics, but others deny such a seemingly "automatic" evaluative capacity.

However variegated its definition, conscience carries with it a prodigious weight and authority. "Freedom of conscience" is a kind of shibboleth in our culture. Doing something "for the sake of conscience" (an old phrase in our language) implies a formidable sanction, one that is almost self-justifying. Something done "in good conscience" has a *prima-facie* case going for it, whereas something done "in bad conscience" portends corruption. The word "conscience" is a common and forceful word in our moral vocabulary. A systematic ethics must attempt to clarify its meanings.

Etymologically, "conscience" comes to us from the Latin *conscientia*, a word that is translated in two distinct ways in English: "conscience" or "consciousness." This dual meaning of *conscientia* evolved gradually as we came to reserve "conscience" for the moral sphere, devising the term "consciousness" for the nonmoral field of awareness. In *Conscience and Its Right to Freedom*, Eric D'Arcy points out: "In Greek, as in Latin and French, a single word serves both purposes; one is left to decide from the context whether or not in a given place it has a moral connotation." In English, moral awareness has its own unique verbal standing in the word "conscience."

Conscience is moral consciousness at work. Our definition of conscience is this: *Conscience is the conscious self as attuned to moral values and disvalues in the concrete.* It is the individual's actual state of sensitivity or insensitivity to the worth of persons and their environment. It is moral orientation toward value. The term "conscience" does not describe the activity of persons as they speculatively contemplate moral issues in which they are not involved. The term has a reference to the concrete order of experience in which the self is existentially implicated. One does not have a conscience problem about someone else's moral quandary unless one is involved in that quandary in some way.

One's conscience, one's moral consciousness, can be sympathetic and become involved simply by considering an ethical case. Affectivity is not excluded and pure detachment from any human problem is unlikely. It is easy and natural for us to be implicated in value questions when we study them and feel their relevance to our own moral situations. Because conscience is the awareness of moral reality, it is aroused when one perceives moral truth. But conscience is not just a matter of intellectual knowledge, of "knowing" that some things are right or wrong. A good conscience is a cultivated heart-felt knowledge, an affective awareness of moral value. It is like an acquired, learned instinct, fallible but instructive.

The key to understanding conscience is to see it as the conscious self in the actual state of moral awareness. This perception necessitates both a knowledge of the moral history of the self and a critical assessment of how the elements of ethical method are represented in the workings of conscience. As spontaneous as it might appear, conscience implies ethical reflection or, at least, some moral foreknowledge. Regarding our wheel model of ethical method, we need to stress that conscience should, with increasing sensitivity and thoroughness, represent all the evaluational elements appropriated by the valuing person. Nicolas Berdyaev is correct when he says that ethics should be "a critique of pure conscience." Conscience is not so much one of the parts of ethics as it is an ethical method embodied in a person. Ethics should seek to purify not just reason but all that a morally evaluating self is, and that includes *all* the evaluational resources of the ethical wheel model. Conscience is best served when an ethics is as complete as possible. Ethics should help conscience to become as fully conscious of moral reality as one can be.

Conscience is not an extraneous imposition on one's moral personality. There is a conscience in every one of us, although in varying degrees of development. Conscience is rooted in the foundational moral experience into which no one who approximates human normalcy is totally uninitiated. As we have seen in chapter 1, the foundational moral experience consists of an appreciation of the value of persons and their environment on this nourishing earth. Conscience grows out of the process of this humanizing experience. No two processes will be identical and neither will any two consciences. But they will not be so totally different that we cannot find agreement on various issues.

Conscience always bears the distinguishing marks of each person's unique moral history. However, every conscience has something fundamentally in common with all others. Each has its roots in the core of the foundational moral experience. Although a developed conscience is not innate in us, the human potential for relating to others and to moral value is. Conscience gives form to this potential and to our natural status as social, morally conscious beings. It is the product of our decisions, education, and formative personal encounters.

Relating Conscience to the Art/Science of Ethics...

Good conscience involves a conscious concern for all the various elements represented by the hub and spokes of the wheel model. To illustrate the point, let us briefly turn to the ethical method in this book, and see how conscience relates to the whole method we have been unfolding.

First, conscience relates to the reality-revealing questions in the expository phase of ethics. The consciences of persons are marked by greater or lesser empirical sensitivity. If we have the habit of inquisitiveness in the face of moral decisions, our conscience will be marked by a readiness to ask and pursue questions. If we have experience with diverse moral issues, we will be better able to perceive distinctions when there are differences. The hub of the wheel model is intended to enhance the empirical sensitivity of conscience by helping us develop the skill to pursue the right questions. The morally inquisitive mind is a prerequisite to the growth of conscience and can prepare us to meet our many decisions that are nearly instantaneous. The more we are conscious of the expository questions — the *what*, the *why*, the *how*, the *foreseeable effects*, and so forth — the more astute questioning is "second nature" to us, the better alerted we are to moral circumstances and the better is our conscience.

Unfortunately, some moral problems do not give us the time to sit down and systematically pursue at leisure all the reality-revealing questions, or to be systematically attentive to the role of the spokes. A well-educated conscience can help us here. It is an acquired moral awareness that includes an ability to respond to the immediacy of situations because it has indeed become second nature to the morally prepared self. Like the creative mind, conscience too must be prepared to respond to moral urgency. Thus the more we reflect ethically, the greater chance do we have to act in good conscience.

The growth of conscience also relates to the evaluational phase of ethics. Because the spokes enable us to be critically aware of the personal and social resources that enter into moral decision making, conscience should embody the moral awareness that we gain through the proper use of each spoke.

For example, the spoke on *creativity* should play a vital role in the stimulation of one's conscience. As the morally conscious self, conscience should exemplify this distinctively human capacity. The developed conscience is not a judge that sits and passes verdicts of right and wrong on situations as they arise. Rather, it shows a responsive awareness and attitude toward the moral possibilities buried in a situation. Good conscience has the skill of discovery and inventiveness. Animated by a creative spirit, it has the strength to discern alternatives in moral situations where the less creative would be at a loss.

Conscience is a virtue, the virtue of moral perceptiveness. It is the cultured and skilled attitude of the mind to perceive what is morally right and to act on it. This virtue forms the basis of the word "conscientiousness." Conscience is the personalized awareness that we are indeed more than the total of the social influences that condition our attitudes and behavior. Through a living conscience we can realize that there are times when we can rise up against societal standards, as many persons with good conscience did in Nazi Germany and in the early civil rights movement in the United States. Developed conscience endows us with the courage of moral dissent and with the hope that moral perception will be effected in others. Conscience is a developed awareness of the foundational moral experience, of the mystery of the moral worth of persons and their environment. It is the force that will save this planet if saved it is to be. Conscience is the force that should animate all human institutions. In fact, it is the only thing that marks them out as "human." Machines can be efficient; only persons can be conscientious.

On Always Following One's Conscience...

If conscience is so esteemed, if it is so ethically important and central, is it always right to follow one's conscience? Can we always be certain that our consciences are right or even well formed? These questions have bothered ethicists for centuries. The question of always following one's conscience surfaces implicitly in a lot of contemporary rhetoric about the rights of conscience, implying that an individual conscience has absolute rights above all others.

The questions and the ideas contained here are misleading. Obviously it can be said, at least in a general way, that one must act in accord with one's conscience. Conscience is not something we change willy-nilly like TV channels. If we are conscientiously convinced that something is morally wrong, we should avoid it; if we are conscientiously convinced that something is morally right, we should act on it. If conscience is the conscious moral self, contradicting it in behavior would violate one's own integrity and be an assault on one's moral convictions. Not to act in accord with one's conscience would cause within the personality that painful fissure called guilt. From this point of view, then, it is always right to follow one's conscience.

But there are misleading implications in the notion of *always following one's conscience*. The idea might not suggest sufficient recognition of the fact that conscience is fallible. Human beings are fallible. Ethics is fallible and so too is conscience. This fact should prompt some reservations about the absolute hegemony of conscience. Conscience is not to be conceived of as an independent supreme court with irrefutable judicial powers that must always be followed and never criticized by oneself or others. Many evildoers and fools act "in good conscience." We can fool ourselves with a conscience that has been seduced and conscience can become a slave of self-serving rationalization. Conscience should not avoid looking into moral matters as honestly and as fully as possible. It should also be attentive to the evaluative qualities of *affectivity* and *group experience*.

Good conscience has powerful antennae and is regularly alerted to the signals available to it from our counterparts in the community of persons. Conscience is not just "individual" in us. It is also social. Genuine conscience lives in dialogue. It is indeed in conscience that *the one* takes its stand vis-à-vis *the many*, but the individual and personal nature of conscience does not mean *me* against *them*. It means *me* distinct from *them* but intrinsically and naturally *with them*. To the general statement that one should always follow one's conscience it should be added that one should also always question one's conscience. Conscience is not completely autonomous. No conscience is an island.

Do Societies or Institutions Have Consciences?...

Though conscience is primarily a term of personal moral consciousness, we can speak of the conscience of a society or nation. This adaptive use of the term would refer to those distinguishable traits that mark a society with notable sensitivities or insensitivities. We speak, in a similar way, of the character of a people. Certain moral values seem to be more highly prized in some cultures than in others and in some professions than in others. In looking to a nation's awareness of moral values, that is, in looking to a nation's conscience, one would naturally seek to discern its attitudes toward other nations with different values. Individual freedom, for example, enjoys high esteem in American society, a notion that contributes to an American attitude toward countries with contrary norms. The legal profession is understandably marked by a highly developed sense of due process and fair play. The study of group conscience is of considerable usefulness, since individual conscience will, to a great extent, reflect the strengths and weaknesses of the group. It is sometimes easier to get perspective this way and to admit moral weaknesses when we see them in their communal context.

15

Conscience and Guilt

Conscience looks forward and backward; it also takes on the challenges offered in the present. It can be a source of joy and exuberance when our behavior enhances moral meaning and when it achieves the rich potentials of personhood. But probably it is in looking back in pain that we experience conscience so vividly; so we will give the backward look of conscience special attention.

The feelings that accompany the awareness of guilt seem to be the most perceptible manifestations of conscience. The term "remorse," from the Latin *mordere*, meaning "to bite," is often used to describe the experience of guilt. (The Middle English phrase "agenbite of inwit," meaning "conscience biting against one's self," might have been a more direct way of expressing it.) As the etymology of the words "remorse" and "agenbite" suggests, the experience is not a happy one. Guilt is the product of a split between what we basically know to be good and what we do or fail to do instead. (For our purposes here, we are using the terms "guilt" and "guilt feelings" interchangeably.) If conscience means moral awareness, guilt is failure to act morally when the moral is perceived. Guilt may be a fundamental, universal human experience; but since the Freudian revolution in psychology, guilt is often treated as a symptom of illness, an understanding that can be misleading. There is unhealthy guilt, of course. Some might feel the agony of remorse when there is really no objective reason. Such guilt is like a red light that flashes on a dashboard when nothing is wrong. That kind of guilt requires therapy. Realistic guilt compares to the light that flashes when something *is* wrong. We ignore it at our own peril.

The loss of the unity between moral perception and action is the first cause of remorse. A saying of Goethe gives further insight: "All laws and rules of conduct may ultimately be reduced to a single one: to truth." Untruth is unsettling. The ancients used to say that "the liar pays the price" (*nemo gratis mendax*). This principle is behind the mechanism of the "lie detector" or polygraph. Truth is ultimately native to us; falsehood is a disturbing alien. Without underestimating the human capacity to naturalize this alien, we can appreciate the inherent congeniality of truth to human consciousness. When untruth

is materialized in our attitudes and behavior, the process of humanization is stunted. What we do is not true to what we are and must
become. Recognition of this lack of unity is the disturbing experience
of objective guilt — objective because there is real reference to moral
reality. Guilt is a response to the contradiction of the foundational
moral experience that sees the link and unity between the value of self
and the value of others. Thus guilty behavior recoils upon ourselves.
The offended value is ours *as well as* that of other persons.

Three Notions of Guilt...

There are at least three major ways in which guilt is understood: (1) in
a taboo sense, (2) in an egoistic sense, or (3) in what we will argue
is the realistic sense. Because one's view of guilt will also reflect the
presuppositions of one's ethics, each of these ways reflects a different
conception of ethics and conscience.

Taboo Guilt. Guilt at the taboo level is a primitive appreciation that
sees something as wrong because it is forbidden. Guilt here is the violation of a prohibition that may or may not make sense. Making sense
is not of the essence for the taboo mentality, and neither is it essential
that the behavior judged wrong be harmful. Taboo behavior is wrong
regardless of the good or harm that it might do. This "regardless" is the
crux of the matter. The behavior is wrong not because it harms or
because of the circumstances, but simply because it is forbidden. The
forbiddenness is superimposed upon the situation; it comes from without and not from an assessment of moral circumstances. It might be
morally good and reasonable to do that which is forbidden, but that
is radically irrelevant to taboo, which is sweeping and undiscriminating in its scope. That which is under taboo is not open to nuance or
distinction. Guilt as taboo involves transgression that leaves one liable
to the sanctions of "the powers that be," however these powers may
be perceived. The mind under the control of taboo does not do ethics
and it does not serve conscience well. It simply shies away from target
areas that have been designated by certain beliefs as dangerous.

Taboo in its origins, however, might represent a great deal of discernment. We are accustomed to think of taboo in association with
the inexplicable prohibition of primitive peoples. There can be two
mistakes in doing that. First, taboo is not limited to illiterate cultures.
It does occur in modern dress. And, second, taboo is not entirely inexplicable in its origins. Some particular prohibitions among peoples with
whom our acquaintance is imperfect may remain unexplained; others
appear to be the product of ignorant superstition and nothing more.
But we ought not presume one or the other. The taboos of primitive
peoples may be reflective of what society judged necessary for its survival and welfare. Many taboos that forbade certain foods or activities

were literally lifesaving and the fruit of long and dire experience. Other taboos, such as the almost universal incest taboo, seem to arise from a recognition of the biologically and socially disruptive force of intrafamilial sexual relationships. Although elements of a realistic ethics might be discerned in the development of taboo, the problem is that taboo is undiscriminating. Once it is established, the door is closed to important distinctions. Taboo does not make distinctions when there are differences. Thus it becomes a substitute for ethics. When taboo is operating, we can anticipate that unlikely arguments will be brought forth in an attempt to justify it.

Modern taboo, a phenomenon to which we should be intellectually alert, will not always come equipped with elaborate rationalizations. One should look for it in patterns of conduct that are well ensconced within our social structures and history. A full analysis of issues such as sexism, racism, the moral rights of patients, attitudes toward sexuality, the ideologies of nationalism and classism would uncover a number of unnatural and gratuitous prohibitions within socially accepted moral perspectives. Discussions about the evil of "flag burning" are suggestive of taboo thinking. Modern dress codes also exemplify the power of taboo. The professions, too, are heavy with taboos, not all of which make sense.

Egoistic Guilt. Beyond the level of taboo, guilt may be understood in an egoistic way. The motive in egoistic guilt is antiseptic in nature and involves an excessive concern for one's own moral purity and integrity. "Decent people don't do that" is an example of this kind of thinking, the implication being that "decency," however conceived, is the all-controlling concern. Guilt is here perceived as a personal disfigurement. Doing something wrong means damaging yourself in some fashion. It is not a question of whether something in its context is harmful, but of whether it is in your best interest. The risk factor of getting caught with the possibility of suffering negative consequences becomes more important than the morality of an issue. Egoistic guilt shows a mindset that is ultimately "me-centered." In cases of terminal illness, for example, decisions are often made not according to the rights or wishes of the dying person but according to the guilt feelings others would have by allowing the person to die. Egoistic guilt interferes with what might be morally right.

This form of guilt proceeds from a self-centered ethics that involves a desire to avoid real moral responsibility. In effect, it is an effort to stay within acceptable limits so as not to be blamed or hurt. Egoistic guilt also shows itself in the attitude of doing what one must do to avoid getting caught. It looks for loopholes and is minimalistic in avoiding moral accountability. Egoistic guilt is based on a selfishness that lacks a full framework of moral responsibility.

Realistic Guilt. Finally there is an understanding of guilty behavior
that we can call "realistic." Realistic guilt is *conscious and free behavior
(active or passive) that does real, unnecessary harm to persons and/or their
environment.* In speaking of conscious and free behavior, we acknowledge the number of unconscious determinisms that are a fact of our
psychic lives. We are free only to a point. "Conscious and free" refers
to the fact that human behavior that cannot be linked to any conscious
control or freedom falls outside the realm of moral accountability.

Behavior can be active or passive, that is, it may take the form of
commission or omission. Describing it as passive should not give the
impression that it denotes the complete opposite of activity. Omission
can be quite voluntary and influential. There was, for example, a case
in Germany when a husband and wife had a serious quarrel. In a rage
the husband hanged himself in the presence of his wife. The case went
to law. On the face of it, it would seem that the wife could not be
charged with anything. She had simply witnessed a suicide. However,
the court did not stay with this surface rendition of the facts. It noted
that the wife could easily have cut her husband down and that, as Helen
Silving explains in her article "Euthanasia: A Study in Comparative
Criminal Law," she was "satisfied with the course of events — events
which had occurred without any action on her part." Silving continues
to explain that the wife was convicted of the crime of "failure to render
assistance." As a subsequent court consideration put it, according to
Silving, "In omitting to act, contrary to duty, she failed to interrupt
the chain of causation started by her husband; she thereby participated
in causing his death."

The difficulty of delineating how this woman "participated in causing his death" in the course of events "which had occurred without
any action on her part" strains the minds of jurists and ethicists. Yet
the direction of German law in this regard seems sound. When we do
not do anything about that which we *can* do something, it is distinctly
different from situations in which we do not do anything about that
which is beyond our influence. The question then becomes whether we
should do something when we *can* do something. The answer to that
will reflect a number of things but will always reflect one's basic sense
of what persons are and what they deserve.

An omission may of course represent momentary psychological
paralysis so that it would scarcely qualify under the category of conscious and free behavior. It may also represent heightened and intense
personal decision. The husband who would like to be married to someone else and who *omits* going for the medicine when his wife manifests
signs of a heart attack is not really in the position of "having done nothing." What he had "done" is *an act of refusal* that is free and highly
significant. This refusal might in fact be the most voluntary action of

his life. In most actions we are buoyed by habit, social expectations, or inner determinisms. In this instance the husband might be summoned to an agonizing activation of his freedom of the sort that he may have rarely if ever before experienced. His own deliberate volition will be called for in a unique way. His behavior is *passive* in the sense that it is not as active as it would be if he were to shoot his wife, but it is *active* in the sense that it is free, conscious, and effective volition. Deliberate omission is not outside the circle of human moral responsibility.

There are also "good omissions" that illustrate the active, volitional quality of some omissions. A doctor might, out of fear of a lawsuit, order massive resuscitory efforts (a "code") for a hopelessly ill patient who is dying in terrible agony. When the "code" signal is sounded, some nurses might respond with all deliberate slowness so that the "code" fails and the patient dies. Their omission of the usual speed was based on an assessment that the patient was beyond healing and that the "code" would only extend the dying in a painful and unreasonable way. In such a case, what they did *not* do was more willful and effective than were the few things they did in their deliberately delayed reaction to the emergency call. Their omissions were most morally significant.

Not all omissions are equally deliberate. Some are distinguished by a high degree of conscious awareness of what could have been done but was not. Sometimes morally significant omissions are clouded by ignorance or by a diminished awareness of what is being left undone. Our omissions regarding problems we know nothing of and could know nothing of are simply *amoral*. We do not have moral responsibility for that of which we are truly ignorant.

The idea of moral ignorance is more subtle and significant, however. We can have what can be called a "masked conscience" in which ignorance is contrived and self-servingly sustained. But then, because it represents a choice, it is not so much ignorance as avoidance. The morally demanding reality is dimly perceived and then instinctively commended to the shadows of the mind. This point may be illustrated by many affluent Americans who have a kind of masked unawareness of the deep poverty existing in various places in this country. The number of homeless children in this country equals the population of Denver. More than one half of all African American children are born into poverty. Studies repeatedly show all this is related to national policies, and yet little guilt is felt for any of this by the citizens. Our broad unawareness of world hunger illustrates the same problem. The "ignorance" of "good" white people of the indignities visited upon certain minorities is another example. In a crucial way, this kind of affected ignorance falls under the broad understanding of "conscious behavior." It has its own kind of determined deliberateness, even though it is obviously not that of a first-degree murderer. If the ignorance involved is total there is no guilt. We are outside the area of conscious behavior. But the ignorance of the examples just cited is more likely a self-serving artefact.

Omissions are morally significant because they "show where the heart is." They reveal the morally crucial center of sensitivity that shapes attitudes and character. The things we do often support the character image that we wish to project. But the undone deed speaks loudly of how much caring animates one's moral existence, of how deeply one is into the foundational moral experience, and of how one's priorities are set. Omission can also show an undergirding apathy and, on the collective level, a nonresponse to the legitimate moral claims that confront a society. In the realistic definition of guilt, then, "behavior" refers to both omission and commission.

Guilty behavior does *real, unnecessary harm*. "Harm" is the critical term here. If we do no real harm (psychological or physical), we incur no guilt. When speaking of taboo, we noted that it often has realistic origins. Taboo represents an aversive reaction to perceived harm and finds expression in an absolutized way that allows for no discriminating judgment. Because it does not allow for distinctions when there are differences, taboo becomes unreal; it bans whole categories of human behavior with no regard for differentiation, even though in certain instances certain activities do no *real, unnecessary harm*. This kind of nondiscriminatory thinking is the central failure of taboo, or of any kind of ethics that abstractly condemns all behavior of a certain type. The point here is not that you cannot theorize about guilty action. To do just that is a prime task of ethics. The problem arises when a theory has no empirical base. Then that which is called wrong might be harmful only to the theory. Hence the need to insist on *real harm* in the definition of guilty behavior.

The objection, of course, can be raised that we put too much weight on the notion of harm. In response, we would say that harm to persons and/or their environment is the nether side of the good, and the whole of ethics is geared to the exploration of this bipolar reality. Ethics is concerned with the systematic discernment of what does or does not befit the complex reality of human behavior. To say that it explores good and evil is to say the same thing. To assess the real, unnecessary harm involved in a particular situation may be exceedingly difficult and admit of only imperfect success, but it is a task from which the valuing animal cannot hide. The alternative would be to surrender meaningful forms of human activity to chance. The difficulties involved in doing ethics and assessing harm amid the boggling intricacies of collective life, such as the political and the commercial, have driven many to treat moral concern and ethics as though it had meaning only amid the home and hearth issues of personal, private lives. This retreat is an intellectual and moral defection that shrinks the meaning of life and avoids the complexities of real human issues. The most important moral decisions are made at the corporate and political levels of life.

The term "unnecessary" has to qualify harm in the definition of guilty behavior because it is sometimes moral and necessary to cause harm. Killing in self-defense when there are no less drastic alternatives is obviously harmful to the deceased. It may, however, be judged *necessary* harm. The apportionment of goods and bads in a society may do necessary harm to certain citizens. Police officers who take capital risks to protect people are open to terrible harm. They are not, however, doing evil, as an Ayn Rand might like to think, in risking this harm. The circumstances may show it to be necessary. Similarly, the quota system that gives preferential treatment to groups that have suffered unfair discrimination can be another example of justifiable necessary harm to some. If the system works well and all the talent of the nation is released to the benefit of all, the harm sustained by some in the process may be seen as reasonable and moral. It is not *unnecessary harm* and it is not evil. Put another way, the greater harm is in sustaining the unreasonable monopoly.

It may be all too obvious to say that wrongful behavior is so because it is harmful to *persons*. Less obvious is the "and/or their environment" part of the definition. This environment includes plant life, animals, minerals, air, and all the other elements that make up our terrestrial *and* extraterrestrial context. Our moral universe stretches to everything that human behavior touches, and this now includes the adjacent portions of the physical universe. Like individuals who strike it rich and arrogantly abandon their kith and kin, as we alluded to in chapter 2, *homo sapiens*, having evolved into a conscious and somewhat free animal, treats the earth as though it were a stage that has no intrinsic connection with the drama played upon it. We forget that we grew up out of the material of that stage and that we are still filially related to it. We should show deep respect toward our roots and parent earth.

The Problem of Collective Guilt...

Various notions of collective guilt have come to the fore in the past few decades. With the realization that a good deal of corporate and political agency is wrongful, the question of assigning guilt is a problem that is with us. Who is guilty of the cruel extravagances of war? Who, more specifically, was guilty for the massacre at My Lai? The generals, Lieutenant Calley, the Congress who provided the monies to wage the war, or we who provided the Congress? Who is guilty for the wasting of the earth wrought by corporate power? The board of directors, the stockholders, those who buy the products of those corporations? Can guilt be inherited? Do we bear the guilt of our forebears who in centuries of dishonor drove the Native Americans from their home-lands and slaughtered many of them? Is reparation owed to women and African Americans because of the damaging discrimination that has been visited upon them? Is collective guilt a motivating factor be-hind terrorist activity? How can the innocent of a larger national or ethnic group be perceived as guilty? Is there such a thing as guilt by association? Can some be more guilty than others? Simply put: How well founded is collective guilt?

This notion seems to be as old as the mythologies that deal with an original human fall that adversely affects everybody, but when trying to explicate the precise meaning of collective guilt, we may never be fully satisfied. How can everybody be guilty? Is everyone equally guilty? In one sense, if everyone is guilty, no one is guilty. If so, collective guilt is a vicious notion that would absolve groups of all moral responsibility. Since most good and most harm is done by groups, it would not be helpful to remove them from all moral judgment and responsibility.

Is it not the *individual* who acts, even if the individual is acting in a group with other actors? Are we not individually responsible for the actions we perform, even in groups? Collective guilt does not seem to discriminate. Further, it can be something for people to wallow in, comforted by the conviction that there is nothing much that can be done about it since collective moral responsibility is such a morass. Collective guilt can be a species of self-serving rationalization. But in spite of all these objections, a proper understanding of collective guilt seems feasible.

Justice as the Key to Collective Guilt...

Collective guilt is possible because we have a social nature. We are in society because we are social beings, not because of an arbitrary con-tract. It is not just an optional arrangement; it is us. There is a social as well as a private, personal dimension to our being. We do indeed agree to certain kinds of social structuring and find utility in social living, but such facts are subsequent to our constitutional sociality as persons. Our conception of guilt cannot be atomistically individualis-tic. Our natural relatedness to others must show through in our guilt as well as in the collective virtue of our social structures.

As a group or a society, we allow for the emergence and permissi-bility of certain kinds of activities and attitudes. In his article "Guilt: Yours, Ours, and Theirs," Theodore R. Weber writes: "We are not pas-sive or neutral toward the social housing we inhabit. We receive it, use it, reinforce it, and pass it on." If as a people we have a character that reflects the collective make-up of all, regardless of the diversity of backgrounds, we share a common responsibility. In this respect there is a complicity in our systemic arrangements and in the actions that we permit (or omit) in the name of others. If individuals can act or fail to act collectively, they can be collectively guilty.

To clarify further an understanding of collective guilt (and to address the question at the end of the last chapter — Do Societies or Institutions Have Consciences?), we can refer to chapter 3 where we discussed the three kinds of justice that mark our relationship with others: individual, social, and distributive. Individual justice is between individuals or discrete groups; social refers to the debt of the individual to society, and distributive to the obligations of the social whole to the individual. A full understanding of the value of persons integrates the three kinds of indebtedness implied in the three kinds of justice. Since justice and the value of persons can be denied at any level, guilt, correspondingly, can occur at any level.

Of course, it is easier to imagine and conceptualize violations of individual justice. John cheats James in a business deal. Simple enough. We are less accustomed to thinking of how we are unjust as a group. By not paying our debts of concern and involvement to the common good, by allowing social evils to continue without any slight effort through personal activity or through groups to which we belong, we contribute to social injustice. Slavery could not have existed without a lot of complicity and apathy. So too for a number of social ills today. How many men could say that they have done enough to work against the effects of sexism in our society and in our institutions and professions?

As moral and ethical beings, we must work for conditions in which justice will be the critical social energy. Obviously, we are a long way from such an achievement. To say that we are guiltless is to say that we are just; it is to say that we are morally sensitive and caring and creative enough.

Collective guilt arises from what is undone in a society and not only from what a society does wrong; it is a communal omission of appropriate moral response. But this omission is something for which the individuals in the group *are* responsible. Yet, it is not something that could be tried in a court of law. Its proper forum is conscience. In certain instances, as we have seen, the failure to render assistance in a particular case can be made a matter of judicial concern when the opportunity to aid is clear and individualized. Unfortunately, communal guilt allows for no such precision, and yet it is a critical fact of human life and the cause of most of our problems.

It would seem that the enthusiastic malevolence of the lynch mob appears in subtle disguise in human society more often than we would care to admit. This grim side of our history is something that must be included in an estimate of collective guilt. We have a predisposition not just for grouping, but for grouping against, and the group gives strength to our baser proclivities. In a face-to-face encounter with all its chastening immediacy, we feel ourselves on the spot. Our reactions are likely to be more benign. But group experience dilutes individual conscience, making it easier to do real, unnecessary harm to persons. To speak only of individual guilt is to miss this influential aspect of our many-leveled reality. Because we are capable in diverse ways of seeing evil and of doing it with some conscious deliberation, we would not know ourselves if we did not know our guilt, collective and individual. But there is such a thing as healthy guilt, guilt that is not neurotic and that calls not so much for therapy as for moral transformation. Part of the force of that transformation is a well developed conscience that ethics must serve.

STUDY QUESTIONS

1. Explain the meaning of conscience and clarify the relationship between ethics, conscience, and the wheel model.

2. If conscience implies moral awareness and perception, how can there be, in good conscience, contradictory conclusions to the same moral problem? Can some consciences be better developed than others? Are all consciences on the same moral level? Is it always right to follow one's conscience? How is conscience related to character?

3. Give examples of conflicts between an individual's conscience and socially accepted norms. How should persons react if they disagree with major policies of their corporate employer? Discuss.

4. If one perceives a moral obligation but does not act or acts wrongly, guilt can arise. Discuss three understandings of guilt and explain how omission as well as commission can be part of individual and collective moral guilt. How can guilt be a healthy psychological and moral phenomenon?

5. Give some examples of contemporary taboos, of egoistic guilt, and of collective guilt. Show some of the forms that taboo takes in modern professions.

6. In reference to collective guilt, evaluate terrorist activity. Are innocent people used as targets of collective guilt or as targets of revenge? On what grounds can terrorist activity be condemned?

7. Give some examples of how we are individually and collectively responsible for the way we treat our environment.

8. Show how an individual's conscience can be shaped by a society. Give some examples. If we passively support unjust social policies, are we in any way guilty?

PART FIVE

Avoiding the Hazards of Moral Discourse

16

Hazards and Pitfalls

A hazard of moral discourse is anything that interferes with moral judgment. The main general hazards are incompleteness and insensitivity, as we have stressed throughout our study of ethics. The ethical wheel model tries to counter these failings. It is designed to give us theoretical clarity, to help us uncover the complexity of moral reality, and to aid us in making well-informed judgments.

Beyond the general hazards of incompleteness and insensitivity, there are seven specific hazards that merit special attention: *myth, cognitive mood, false analogies, abstractions, selective vision, role,* and *banalization.* This list of inherent hazards is illustrative, not exhaustive. Even when we consciously try our best to avoid these hazards, we can still be influenced by them in the way we see and judge moral issues. Reality is not transparent. It is a fallacy to think of the mind as a docile camera or mirror that accurately reflects back to us things as they are. Human knowing is interpretative. We don't just receive; we filter and relate everything new to something old.

What happens when we *know* is that we both receive and give. Knowable reality is not simply ingested as is, unrelated to the rest of our experience. It fits into the overall universe of our past experiences and knowledge. In this respect, knowledge is relational and within a context of meaning. When something new or strange and different comes before us, we try to give it meaning within the context of what we already know. If we cannot, it is frightening, like the proverbial alien from Mars. We *know* by fitting things into a pattern of familiarity. The mind wants to make sense of things. To do this it places a high value on familiarity and it will readily reject what appears meaningless and unrelatable.

Persons arrive at intellectual maturity when, in their search for meaning, they so extend their relational field of knowledge that they overcome the narrowness imposed by hazards. Openness of the mind is the mark of such maturity. But there are always limits to how open our minds are. In our hunger for meaning we may project more than we receive. In such a situation we do not discover meaning — we fabricate it or we accept the fabrication that society has given us. Thus at the outset we need to be aware of anything that impedes moral understanding.

Knowing, therefore, is a hazardous business. Because of our urgent need to make sense, we often impose meaning that is not there. And, on top of that, there are filters and barriers between us and reality. To improve our reality contact, we have to be aware of the obstacles we face. The first, and most potentially damaging, is myth. Myth has many positive meanings, but we are using it here in the sense of a distortional filter.

Myth as Interpreter of Meaning...

To know the ways of moral understanding, ethics must chart out a method. But the best method in the world will do little for someone whose vision of the real is captivated by a distorting myth. A full and sensitive method must recognize the hazards of moral discourse. We do not know solely "from the neck up"; all that we are is involved. We also know out of a history and a social setting. There are filters, in other words, socially and intrapersonally derived, that stand between us and what is. A good ethical method questions those filters in the hope of minimizing their distorting effect.

Myth is the first of such silent but busy filters. Immediately, it is necessary to explain what myth means in this context since, as we have said, it is a polyvalent word. Words are like people in that they have many relatives and hangers-on. When you decide to marry one to your particular purpose, it is wise to make clear in advance that it is the word you want and not the whole family of associations.

Myth in our usage is this: *It is a complex of feelings, attitudes, symbols, memories, and experienced relationships through which reality is refracted, filtered, and interpreted.* By that definition, knowledge is always to some degree mythic. Interpretation will always be affected by the complex of our feelings, attitudes, and so forth. Sometimes this will be gainful. Buoyed by a creative myth, persons may rise to heights they never would have aspired to in the absence of the myth. The confidence-inspiring myth of "American know-how" has historically served to keep our technologists working to the point of success when those working without the myth would have given up at an earlier more "reasonable" point. The myths surrounding patriotism and parenthood often bring forth generosity and imagination from the most unlikely subjects. Myths may be the vehicle of ideals that keep persons and societies moving forward. They can be described in very positive terms. But if myths limit moral cognition, they become a hazard and all the thinking done under their sway becomes impaired. Our concern here is with myth in this pejorative sense, as a limiting force in moral awareness.

Myths are historical and social in their roots. We might think of a private myth developed in the history of one person, but this is not the common usage of the term. Normally when we speak of myth, we refer to a phenomenon that is (or has been) present and operative in the culture. Myths are the way collectivities find identity, the way they interpret and give meaning to things. All cultures are under the influence of myths. The myth of woman is an example. Although this myth is being brought under social criticism in many cultures today, it is ingrained in much of what we do and think. If we look at it closely, it can instruct us on many of the basic properties of myth.

Often social, historical, and biological exigencies lay the foundations for myth. Because a man does not get pregnant and cannot nurse a baby, he appeared to be the more natural candidate to leave the cave and go forth to meet the challenges of the outside world. What eventually emerged was the myth that a woman is essentially a creature of the home. Cooking and children are the realities that define her and accurately reflect her true identity. Although some attitudes are slowly changing, the unmarried woman is still unlike her counterpart, the bachelor, who is not seen as a truncated person because of his single state. She, however, is too generally seen as lacking the reality that symbolizes the meaning of her myth. A woman is defined, according to this myth, not by her professional responsibilities or personal qualities and talents but by her domestic relationships.

The myth of woman also illustrates the fact that myths can be complex and converge into an explanation of historic reality. For instance, the myth of woman associates the feminine with temptation and the origins of evil and it can be found in the larger context of cosmogonic myths that imaginatively and poetically recount human origins. Woman does not fare well in many of the larger myths. Relating an account given by Sappho and Hesiod, the fourth-century Latin commentator Servius wrote that "Prometheus is said to have stolen fire and revealed it to men. The gods were angered by this and sent two evils on the earth, women and disease."

The power of myth lies in the fact that it can affect you without your knowing it. The myth is in you. The filter is in place, and reality dashes against it, is repelled, and does not get into your mind. That we can be so inured to them makes them treacherous. Even now we are inured to the de facto segregation of women from government and many professions where males predominate with lopsided majority.

Myths are stubborn. They are resistant to data that do not square with their interpretation. They can also be a shield for guilt. They may conveniently cover over some ugly facts that might require painful moral conversion. To attack a myth is to attack well-established vested interest. Not only will guilt be exposed but privileges lost. Myths also interlock with other myths and this gives them added strength.

Disturbing one myth might disturb other advantageous myths and this can make us defensive and protective of our myths. There are strong emotional commitments to myths, commitments that will not be unsettled simply by logical criticism. And if myths are tinged with a religious ideology, the whole foundation of our sense of reality is affected. Religiously braced myths are the most unyielding.

The etiology of the myth of woman is more complex than we could suggest in this brief treatment, but clearly this historic myth shows how profoundly the mind can be bewitched by myths. Since the power of myth is frightening, some deliberate fear of it is the mark of the wise. *A critical consciousness of myth is essential to ethics.* The task here for ethics is never-ending. If we manage to critique and dislodge a deleterious myth, we are likely to substitute another for it or develop a counter-myth such as the super-woman/super-mom ideal. Unfortunately, as many persons are realizing, no one can *do* and *have* it all. The mythic call to be a super-mom is unrealistic. Frustrations under this kind of myth are bound to happen. As we demythologize, we remythologize. Criticism may at least yield better myths, and fruitful myths may succeed bad ones. But since all myth is marked by stereotypical thinking, all myths call for criticism.

All professions are heavy in myth. In the medical profession, for example, there are myths about the power of a physician, the role of a nurse, and the meaning of being a patient. Because of these myths, authority is taken from the patient (who, when informed, should have the last word) and given to the medical professionals. The patients are victims of the myth too and they do not even think they have a right to make their own important decisions. Business persons also operate out of myths and this often hurts their entrepreneurial effectiveness. Very often, highly paid consultants and "motivational experts" are merely helping people escape their demonic myths and do what would have been the obviously right thing were it not for the blinding myth.

The power of myth to stereotype is the power to lock our thought patterns into undifferentiated abstractions that prevent us from assessing specific moral circumstances. Mythic thinking distorts our perception of concrete reality. For example, in the psycho-political world that we all live in, stereotypical thinking abounds in the propaganda that various parties and nations use to govern opinion. (Propaganda is always pregnant with myth.) Sometimes stereotypes reinforce biased attitudes, and when allied to fears, they create a world where symbols replace experience and where differences become threats. Because knowledge in the psycho-political universe is so heavily mediated, myths and stereotypes have easy access to the mind. Even though they can change from one generation to the next, they are forcefully operative in our judgment of diverse groups and nations. What is required by sound ethics is the recognition of the mythic bent of our knowing. However, it is no simple matter to get a critical view; it always seems easier to criticize someone else's myths. Myth can also relate to the notion of "ideology," but the latter term implies a different kind of thought process. Ideologies, of course, contain myths and to some degree marshal them into the work of understanding and organizing collective movements. Ideology involves a rational and systematizing element that differs from myth. Ideology is a somewhat systematic way of making sense of reality. There are ideologies of capitalism and socialism. American "messianism," which sees the United States as the solution to all world problems, is a stubborn enduring ideology. Ideology and myth both can lead us to prefer our conceptualizations of the reality to reality itself. If morality is based on reality, a discerning ethics must try to get to that reality by working through myths, stereotypes, and ideologies. Looking at hazards of moral discourse, then, is not an optional exercise for ethics.

Cognitive Mood...

A second hazard of moral discourse is cognitive mood. An identical event or physical object will not look the same to a child, a dying person, a lover, a business executive, a poet, a Wisconsin farmer, or a nomad. Neither will any of these persons view that reality in the same unchanging light since moods change. Mood affects the way we perceive and understand, and its influence might at times be all-controlling. Even a child will learn early on that there are times to ask for things and times not to, depending on the mood of the parent. We often sense the impact of mood on others, and we ought not neglect it in ourselves.

Mood is a conditioner of our subjectivity. It can sharpen our vision and make us more sensitive, or it can place a veil between us and reality. A change of mood can induce an apology for something that an earlier mood caused. Mood can be a significant factor in the way we perceive and act. The cognitive effect of mood is not always negative, but when it is it can radically alter how we do ethics and judge moral issues. Since mood is such an omnipresent part of us, it merits consideration among the hazards of moral discourse. Mood casts long shadows over all our valuing, whether those values be aesthetic, commercial, or specifically moral. It is not just the thinking animal that evaluates; it is the thinking, feeling, sensing, believing, reacting, and culturally situated animal that responds to value. The moral person does not operate in a void but in an enormousness of intentional and external contextualizing factors. Mood is a significant aspect of this valuational context.

Mood is broader than myth and cannot be as neatly defined, although it can include myths and be influenced by them. Mood is an affective and intellectual mode of attunement to an environment. It signifies a certain mindset that is reflective of one's personal and cultural orientation. The mood of individuals is not entirely unrelated to the vital matrix of cultural moods around them. A mood reflects the accents within the psychic air. Certain things can be cherished while others go ignored. Paulo Freire's work on *conscientization* opened up the minds of the poor in Latin America to the fact that their deprivation was not an ontological and immutable datum. For this reason, the forces of oppressive government were instinctively shrewd enough to challenge and ban his work, since it would transform the mood of the passive poor whose attitudes and feelings would be radically changed.

The mood of American consumers has changed in recent years and the market has thus been transformed. The mood in American journalism changed with the Watergate experience. It had been accepted practice for journalists to cover over some of the personal peccadillos of politicians. Personal failings were well known to reporters, but would go unreported. That is less likely now. Politicians haven't changed that much but the mood of the press has. In this new mood, journalists perceive the right and even the obligation to reveal whatever they find. The change is in the way they now view political reality.

Mood also arises from salient decisions and commitments that have been made. The Declaration of Independence in many significant ways changed the mood of the colonies; even those who had little enthusiasm for rebellion could not be entirely immune to the lure of the new mood. A deeply felt decision to become committed to a person or cause changes one's mood and perception. Sometimes an already existing mood becomes intensified, as is often the case at political conventions and rallies.

Religion too is a significant mood-maker. The framers of our Constitution, for example, were not just pragmatic students of social planning. They were that, but they also were animated by a religious conception of what humanity is and what it needs. As we discussed in reference to the foundational moral experience (see chapter 2), belief is a normal state of human beings, whether it amounts to religious faith or not. Belief is not limited to formal religion. Even the philosopher or the person of reason is filled with it. We have neither the time nor the power to demonstrate all that we need to accept to make life feasible and possibly good. And, therefore, we believe. There is nothing necessarily irrational in believing. Belief is an achievement of discerning affectivity. It arises from the nonrational field of perception. Though it may be utterly misguided and foolish, it may also have access to truth that reason cannot reach. This fact of our cognitive nature is important for an understanding of mood. What we believe and what we then dare hope for set the tone and create the mood in which we know and evaluate. Those who believe little and hope little will see life through little eyes. Creativity will not be their forte. For if mood relates to the way we feel and perceive, it relates to our creativity.

Though it is true that our decisions and commitments can significantly affect our moods, it must also be said that mood is never entirely of our own making. To some degree it comes upon us for good or for ill and, because it is spontaneous, we normally cannot reason ourselves into one and out of another. Mood arrives and departs at its own pace. It is affected by other people and even by such unmanageable things as weather and climate. Geography and climate, as well as our biological chemistry, are factors that may enter in and shape mood. Climate, for instance, can influence the tempo of life, our choice of symbols, our closeness to or alienation from the earth, and our dependence on technology. All these factors have resonance in the thinking and feeling subject.

Mood also relates to the action-reaction pendulum in human values. Though we are always in search of the elusive center that we call balance, human history is marked by broad and eccentric swings. We move from disdain toward Vietnam War veterans to jubilation over the veterans of the Persian Gulf War. We can move from global messianism to isolational nationalism, from comfort with established values to suspicion of all that is socially structured. What we react against reveals what we stand for, and as we ride the pendulum from one unbalanced view to another, a mood sets in of which we cannot afford to be unaware.

Finally, mood may be ephemeral or enduring. Sometimes it will be of little relevance to our evaluation and represent a very minor epistemological consideration. At other times, it can govern the way we interpret. Ethics must maintain a critical awareness of the reality and strength of mood and must continue to remind us that we are caught in the swirl of enveloping influences. To ignore or fail to assess these influences in our evaluation is hazardous to the way we do ethics and damaging to those who think their path is clear.

False Analogies...

The third hazard deals with faulty comparisons. A false analogy compares two things that are not really similar. It fails to show fundamental differences, making the comparison unfit. Used more for emotional appeal than for insight, it stresses a superficial likeness while neglecting significant dissimilarities. A correct analogy concentrates on a similarity that is essential to the issue; dissimilar aspects are of minor significance.

Almost all knowing is analogical and comparative. As we know, we relate the unknown to the known. That is a fact of our cognitive life. Our experiences give us a fund of references to which the mind turns for enlightening comparison when something new presents itself. And that is good. The problem, however, arises when our analogical knowing is based on false analogues and when we avoid further critical analysis of the comparison. Herein lies the hazard. We can be so impressed with similarities that we overlook the differences. When there are differences, distinctions should be made. It is for this reason that false analogies are hazards of moral discourse and must be given our attention.

Our proclivity to draw too much from comparisons is understandable. For one reason, the mind's appetite for making sense of things is quickly satisfied if that which is new or strange is compared to the known. Our minds are more comfortable with the familiar, especially in moral matters. We often attempt to understand present events by historical analogies or an issue by comparing it with another that we accept and feel comfortable with. Like all that touches on morality, the effects of false analogies are practical and often crucial. Concerning the decision to go into Vietnam, for example, Arthur M. Schlesinger comments: "The generalizing compulsions in our political rhetoric were reinforced by an uncritical addiction to historical analogy." Some of the political rhetoric of the time, filled with references to stopping Hitler after Munich, made it seem that we were not in Southeast Asia but in another time and place. Our initial involvement to liberate Kuwait was likened by some to another Vietnam and Saddam Hussein to Hitler.

Our analogies and metaphors can trick us and convince us that they encapsulate the whole of the matter. Parents might easily use their first child as an analogue for their second without realizing the unique personality of this second child. If the reality of the first becomes the domineering analogue, the potential of their second child might not be fully actualized. Similarly, one business venture might be sidetracked by an infelicitous comparison to an earlier one. The false analogy that beclouds much of the discussion of our moral dominion over our dying implies that mercy death, even in extreme cases where death is accelerated because of unmanageable pain, is an incipient form of genocide. The comparison is, at least, questionable.

What is crucially lost in false analogies is more than just the perspective of the *what?* question. When they gain control, false analogies short-circuit the work of ethics and block the expository phase from presenting the empirical data to the discerning subject. Moral evaluation and judgment will be based more on figment than on fact. When making analogies, the whole of the ethical wheel model should be remembered. The use of false analogies is obviously telling for ethics as it is for any analytical discipline.

Abstractions...

Like analogies, abstractions are essential means of thought. But they are also a hazard of moral discourse. In one sense, to criticize abstract thinking is impossible and contradictory, since we could not do so without using abstractions. Abstraction is vital to theory and reflection. The term "abstract" comes from the Latin *ab*, "from," and *trahere*, "to draw." If we could not draw or pull away from the particulars that surround us, we could develop no generalizations or standards for critical judgment. We would not be able to perceive what might be. If we could not abstract, we would not be able to think and our minds would register only immediate sense data. It is a glory of the mind that it can abstract. Abstracting allows us to go beyond the particular manifestations of the individual reality and enables us to discover what constancies exist in this infinitely variegated universe. These constancies undergird our generalizations and give us a framework for judging particulars.

Our abstracting power is such that we can move away too far from concrete reality and lose contact with it. Abstractions can be so detached from the particular that they become unreal. It is this unreal sense that lexicographers are noting when they list as possible meanings of "abstract" such things as impersonal, removed, separate, abstruse, or insufficiently factual. Ironically, the abstract presentation of truth can often sound impressively learned. Is it not the hallmark of intellectuality? Yet, it can be a form of reality avoidance that may enjoy powerful prestige. Only hard-core reality could serve to embarrass it. However, if the cognitive mood of the time is not all that concerned with the facts, deceptive, fogging abstractions may flourish.

False abstractions relate to the *ought-to-is* fallacy. "The wish is often parent to the thought." Wishful impressions of what "ought to be" can press us to believe that that is what *is*. At the political level, we might suppose that a nation *should* want a democratic system of government, and therefore it *does* want one. With such abstractions in control, it may take a long time to realize that this particular nation may not be ready for democracy. This fallacy of abstractness can so overcome us with what ought to be that we neglect what is. Parents of a genetically damaged child, for example, may fail to appreciate what the child really is, obsessed as they can be with their stricken hopes of what that child ought to have been. Their abstract conception of what should be might overshadow the many beauties that this child may still possess. It would be abstract in the worst sense to say that the birth of a genetically damaged baby is not tragic. Many people defend aborting fetuses with serious genetic diseases. Nevertheless, after the child is born, his or her concrete possibilities must be accepted and brought to full potential. What the child *is* must not be sacrificed to what the child "ought to" be. The ought in that case is abstract; the child is real.

It should be noted, however, that in good abstractions, the ought-to-is process is praiseworthy. When we abstract from the inadequate present and envision better possibilities, we are moving our perception of what ought to be toward new creative being. In proper abstraction the *ought* is a pressure for a transformation into a better *is*.

The Stereotype...

The ought-to-is fallacy shows something that is prominent in the misuse of abstraction, namely, the stereotype. In the stereotype, as in all false abstractions, the specific is blurred in the generic and the existence of genuine variety is ignored. It unrealistically generalizes. For example, there was a great American stereotype hidden in the symbol of the "melting pot." It is well known by now that the various cultural and ethnic branches have not homogenized into some stereotypical "American." Behind the idea of the melting pot was an abstract notion of nation and community that could not brook cultural pluralism and the real diversities that characterize humanity.

Abstractions then can be creative or beguiling. But we are concerned about their negative potential in this chapter. False and detached abstractions can be very attractive and to some minds almost irresistibly so. Abstractions can be cruel and even lethal. "Making love" sounds fairly concrete and specific, but it might be an abstraction that disguises a rather exploitative event. "Acceptable levels of unemployment" might cover over unconscionable failures of imagination in government policies and in relationships between private enterprise and government. "Free trade" sounds like a fine abstraction and does import some values, but it may also conceal a lot of chicanery, as a short trip through history would reveal.

Describing the conditions preceding the Peloponnesian War, the ancient historian Thucydides complained that the meaning of words no longer had the same relation to things. This fact he saw as a major mark of the unrest of that time. If words are the houses of our thoughts and abstractions, good and bad, a study of their use is an analytical necessity. Although understanding is not limited to words (we know and feel more than we could ever say), words are, nonetheless, the most common symbols of what it is we mean. Falstaff quizzically demonstrates this in Shakespeare's *Henry IV,* Part 1. He saw that the good word "honor" was being asked to cover over abstractly some realities that he was not ready to bear. When battle with all its call to glory and honor was imminent, the unimpressed Falstaff soliloquizes after being reminded by Prince Hal that he owes God a death:

FALSTAFF: 'Tis not due yet; I would be loath to pay him, before his day. What need I be so forward with him that calls not on me? Well, 'tis no matter; honor pricks me on. Yea, but how if honor prick me off when I come on? How then? Can honor set to a leg? No. Or an arm? No. Or take away the grief of a wound? No. Honor hath no skill in surgery, then? No. What is honor? A word. What is in that word honor? What is that honor? Air. A trim reckoning! Who hath it? He that died a' Wednesday. Doth he feel it? No. Doth he hear it? No. 'Tis insensible, then? Yea, to the dead. But will it not live with the living? No. Why? Detraction will not suffer it. Therefore I'll none of it. Honor is a mere scutcheon. And so ends my catechism.

The humorous and realistic Falstaff instinctively checked the key words used in time of war. At such times, words function even more than usually as abstract shields covering much that is unsavory and cruel in the concrete. The flight to abstraction is distinguished by a hesitancy to call a spade a spade. "Nuclear deterrence policy" means a readiness to incinerate millions of people. It means genocide, and it also means a bankrupting military budget to finance research, production, and deployment.

Again in the same insidious vocabulary, "taking out a city" means reducing it and its inhabitants to radioactive ash. False abstractions like to hide behind euphemistic terms. "Taking out" has a clean sporting ring to it. A good block in football is described as "taking out" the other player. The euphemism helps the abstraction to conceal what it really intends. Bombing is described as "a defensive ordnance drop," a confused and chaotic retreat as "a retrograde action," and "invasions" as "incursions." Escape and surrender becomes "peace with honor." Civilian casualties become "collateral damage." What would Falstaff say?

Not all abstract euphemisms are mischievous. If we speak of "mercy death" rather than "killing," the phrase is not an abstract cover-up. "Killing" is too unnuanced a term to describe the compassion and truth of the situation. When a patient is already in a painful dying process, the reality of the particular *what* is different and calls for different phrasing. The mischief of false abstractions and euphemisms occurs when they are used to cover up the moral reality of the circumstances.

The moral problems here relate especially to the questioning and expository phase of ethics. False abstractions cut that phase short. They can also relate to the evaluational phase. For instance, they can open the way to deviant uses of creative imagination. Because they *impose* meaning, false abstractions boggle ethics and prevent it from honestly uncovering moral meaning. If modesty rightly befits the ethical enterprise, bad abstractions are arrogant by nature. This phenomenon of false abstractions is a real hazard of moral inquiry and a necessary concern of a sensitive ethics.

Selective Vision...
The fifth hazard that we face in moral discourse is selective vision. What we select to see tells us much about ourselves and what we consider to be morally significant in our lives. In selective vision our attention is fixated on the nonessentials, while the truly important matters are passed by. It gives us the illusion of moral accomplishment. Businesspersons who would never break a local ordinance at home by burning their leaves or by dumping their garbage on the village green can go to work and make clandestine decisions that will pollute the air we breathe and the water we need; all this is done without compunction and with an aura of civil propriety.

The apparent ability to miss moral meaning is all too typical of selective vision. Preoccupation with minutiae is a permanent human problem that ethics must confront. The German chaplains in the Nazi army who were busy warning their troops against sinning with prostitutes are an example of selective vision and misplaced moral emphasis. What we choose to be morally concerned with also needs ethical evaluation. The apparent ability of these chaplains to miss the collective and political meaning of the larger moral issues shows how selective vision can dominate an ethics. When this happens ethics ends up specializing in the picayune and neglects the important moral issues that must be faced. Selective vision does not want its moral tranquility unsettled, but a holistic ethics must do just that.

Role and Banalization...
The last two hazards of moral discourse that merit our special attention are *role* and *banalization*. Related closely to myth and cognitive mood, role refers to the kind of lifestyle associated with a particular function or office an individual assumes. Its implications for ethical method lie in the fact that a particular code of ethics may come along as an unsuspected stowaway when one embarks on a new role. A role is powerful because it is socially and mythically endorsed and because it can create a mood that affects the way we see things. There is, of course, great positive potential here. Selfish persons, for instance, may rise to unpredicted heights of altruism when they assume a new role that implies a benevolent way of life.

It is not hard to think of the carefree and frivolous individual who becomes serious minded and responsible when the new role of parent is experienced. Role can have a morally sobering effect. The psychology might be as simple as that used in making the troublemaker the leader of a group. However, it is with the negative influence of role that we are concerned. A new role may contain a poor code of ethics, and when it does, it becomes a hazard of moral discourse.

The role of a political advisor may make it "natural" to engage in many questionable practices. A news reporter may easily lose discretion and sensitivity when intent on getting a story. The role mentality simply prescribes that this is the way things are done. As a boy begins to play the role of "a man," he may inertly accept the expectations that he will show no fineness or delicacy of taste and that he will abandon the natural resource of tears. Students may see their role as passive receptacles of information, not as active participants in a process of learning and discovery. Some intellectuals may see themselves as above manual labor or some lawyers may be convinced by their established role that idealism is incompatible with their calling. In every case, the bad ethics that may go with a role is a problem, a hazard, that a holistic ethical theory must face.

Regarding *banalization*, the words of the French paleontologist Pierre Teilhard de Chardin are instructive. "What too closely envelops us," he wrote in *The Vision of the Past*, "automatically ceases to astonish us." The truth of this statement is illustrated by the story of two bricklayers. When they were asked what they were doing, one replied: "Laying bricks!" But the other exclaimed: "Building a cathedral!" Banalization is a loss of crucial perspective and failure to perceive as fully as we should. It obstructs our understanding by blunting our sense of wonder and dulling our affective response especially to moral value. A sense of awe, which we discussed in chapter 1, is foundational to the process of moral experience. Banality is the opposite of this ecstasy and awe upon which the moral process is built. Even our routines can sing. Ethics is hampered by those who are deaf to such songs.

Things that we have grown accustomed to can become banal in our eyes; unfortunately, no sphere of human activity is exempt. We can be so used to doing something that we fail to see its significance and we become apathetic. Banality is a mindset that interferes with moral perception by rendering moral meaning trite. No area of morality is ever really trite.

Regarding these various hazards of moral discourse, we repeat that the list is not exhaustive. There are many ways in which human knowing can go astray, and if we do not recognize hazards, we can easily succumb to them. As we mentioned throughout Part Three, each of the evaluative processes and resources represented by the spokes of the wheel model of ethics can be abused and can serve to diminish our contact with reality. Some of these hazards overlap with others and with problem factors treated in the development of the method employed here. We do not apologize for the overlap if it served, as we intended it, to show an undisclosed side of a moral question. The important thing is for ethics to resist the temptation to view its enterprise as transpiring in a vacuum or in a purely objective and uninfluenced way. It transpires in the maelstrom of social and personal history where moral values confront us with the need to do ethics.

IN FINE...

Justice Holmes used to say that science makes major contributions to minor needs. Ethics is the attempt to make at least minor contributions to major needs. Modern persons have been little attracted to the work of ethics even though their technological genius has caused exponential increases in the number of questions requiring ethical judgment. What we have done in these pages is to present the fruit of many years of professional effort to discover how we as the valuing animal should best do our valuing. We have not sought to solve the problems we have introduced, but we have attempted to show how moral problems can best be addressed.

There is no area of human experience that is not the bearer of moral meaning. Ethics seeks to bring method and some completeness to the human conversation on moral values from which no one is dispensed. If it does that even somewhat well, it will serve a world that is, thus far, more clever than wise.

STUDY QUESTIONS

1. Why should ethical method be concerned with hazards of moral discourse? How do hazards relate to the ethical wheel model? How do they interfere with the search for moral understanding? Can you suggest potential hazards other than the ones already given?

2. Identify some American myths operative in our thinking today. How do they influence moral decisions? For example, does the song "America the Beautiful" contain benevolent mythic thinking and how can it affect the way we perceive such questions as pollution, acid rain, and depletion of natural resources?

3. In many significant ways, myth defines reality for us, and it is a major achievement to discover wherein it is unreal. Investigate mythic thinking behind such terms as "jihad," "crusade," "the promised land," "individualism," and "inalienable rights." How are myth and ideology related?

4. How are myths operative in our attitudes toward the homeless and AIDS victims? How are myth and stereotypical thinking related?

5. Show how cognitive mood can influence moral decisions that have political and legal ramifications, such as those dealing with oil exploration, drilling, and transportation, and those dealing with abortion, capital punishment, and immigration laws. Discuss how religion can control mood. Explain how cognitive mood can relate to the ethical questions *when?* and *where?* Could a company have a certain cognitive mood?

6. Explain the danger of false analogies and how such a danger can radically affect moral decisions. Give some examples of abstractions that might be morally needed and some that seem to cover up bad intentions.

7. Show how selective vision, role, and banalization can prevent us from perceiving full moral reality. Use examples.

Glossary

Amoral (non-moral): That which does not fall within the moral realm and which, therefore, cannot be judged good or bad, morally speaking. For example, a chemical mixture considered in itself is amoral or non-moral. However, if the chemical mixture is a drug like "crack" and it is being sold in a schoolyard, the moral dimension arises because human choice is involved. No conscious human choices are amoral.

Conscience: The morally conscious self as attuned to moral values and disvalues in the concrete. It is the individual's actual condition of sensitivity or insensitivity to the worth of persons and their environment.

Consequentialism: Teaches that human actions are good or bad primarily or exclusively in terms of their effects or consequences. It neglects the moral significance of all the other circumstances mentioned in the center or hub of the wheel model of ethics.

Domino Theory: Other images used to convey same idea are the wedge, the camel's nose under the tent, finger out of the dike, the slippery slope, and the parade of horrors. The idea behind these images is that if you allow one exception, others will inevitably follow and moral control will be lost.

Emotivism: The view that moral judgments are nothing more than emotional reactions to particular issues and not statements that could be true or false.

Ethics: The art/science that seeks to bring sensitivity and method to the discernment of moral values, and that addresses the meaning of humanization. Ethics can also be seen as a dialogue conducted by the moral agent between the moral meaning found in principles and that found in the unique circumstances of the case. Ethics is also described simply as the systematic discussion of morality.

Evaluational Phase: That part of the wheel model of ethical method that helps us to examine and judge what the reality-revealing questions have uncovered. The spokes spell out the multiple ways available to us personally and socially to evaluate moral matters. They include: creative imagination, affectivity, reason and analysis, authority, principles, individual and group experience, comedy and tragedy.

Foundational Moral Experience (FME): The experience of the value of persons and their environment. It is the grounding of all moral knowledge, moral reasoning, and ethics. The experience is at root an affective faith experience and it is processual in the sense that it admits of greater or lesser appreciation. It is a faith experience, not in the usual religious sense, but in the sense that we cannot prove the value of persons and of this earth. We *believe* it just as we believe in basic human rights but cannot empirically prove them.

Guilt: A term that describes the state of having transgressed moral boundaries. Guilt is understood in three ways: at the taboo level, something is considered wrong regardless of whether there is resultant harm or unreasonableness; egoistic guilt sees wrongfulness in terms of personal disfigurement, not because of the impact on other persons; realistic guilt is conscious and free behavior (active or passive) that does real, unnecessary harm to persons and/or their environment. The term "collective guilt" is also used. This term is properly employed to describe undue apathy regarding the obligations of social and distributive justice. It is improperly used to imply that a whole people are responsible for certain acts that others have performed, thus denying any personal center of responsibility.

Hazards of Moral Discourse: Anything that interferes with moral judgment. The generic hazards are incompleteness and insensitivity. The seven specific hazards are myth, cognitive mood, false analogies, abstractions, selective vision, role, and banalization.

Immoral: The opposite of morally good.

Intuitionism: The view that a moral quality is known by direct insight or intuition. The moral goodness or badness of a situation is appreciated simply and directly just as one knows the color yellow to be yellow. Intuitionism bypasses the complexity of ethical analysis, assuming that moral knowledge is largely self-evident.

Justice: Justice is the virtue that renders to each his or her own. *Suum cuique* is the classical Latin expression for justice. Justice ensures that all persons receive their minimal essential due. To deny persons justice is, in effect, to deny their humanity. Justice is the minimal expression of the foundational moral experience. There are three forms of justice: *individual*, *social*, and *distributive*. Individual justice renders what is due in relationships between two persons or two social entities. Social justice represents the debts of the individual citizen to the social whole or to the common good. Distributive justice directs the fair allocation of goods, burdens, and duties among the citizens.

Moral: As the opposite of amoral (non-moral) it refers to matters that do fall within the realm of moral adjudication, as in the expression: "This is a moral matter." This means that it is open to moral judgment, whether it will be judged favorably (as moral) or unfavorably (as immoral).

Naturalism: Any ethical theory that tries to reduce ethical concepts to physical or scientific laws and principles. It is reductionistic and ignores the complexity of moral reality and takes no account of the affective component of moral knowledge.

Natural Law: An approach to ethics that stresses that an understanding of human nature governs the formulation and applicability of principles and that what is "natural" in a holistic sense tends to determine what should be moral.

Pendulum Effect: The tendency in social thought to swing from one extreme to the other.

Positivism: A theory holding that truth can be known only through scientific and empirical means.

Principle of Proportionality: Can be considered the master principle in ethics; to decide what is the most valuable choice in complex moral issues, ethics always weighs and balances values and disvalues.

Profanation, Sense of: The moral shock and horror that we feel when persons (and/or our terrestrial environment) are abused or offended. It is shock and withdrawal we feel when the value of life is debased.

Reality-revealing Questions: The center or hub of the wheel model used to uncover all the morally relevant circumstances. These questions are what? why? who? how? when? where? foreseeable effects? viable alternatives?

Relativism: The viewpoint that says that what we call "morally good" is merely socially approved custom. Relativism holds that right and wrong depend on the cultural setting, that there is no objective morality to which all peoples could appeal. Ethical relativism does not exist in a pure state, but it does pervade much thinking in formal ethics and in the popular culture.

Sanctity of Life: A broadly used term to denote the supreme value of life. Primarily an expression of valuation of the dignity of persons. The term is used by adaptation to refer to the value of all forms of life.

Situation Ethics: A theory that says that moral obligation is dictated by the situation alone. This theory is suspicious of absolutes or hard and fast rules or principles. The term is sometimes used negatively as an excessively permissive approach to ethics. Others use it to insist on sensitivity to situational differences. It is also sometimes called "contextualism."

Supreme Sacrifice: Offering one's life for the welfare of others. It is the most dramatic expression of the foundational moral experience and it is revered in the literature of most cultures.

Taboo: Treating certain actions as wrong regardless of the circumstances. The taboo approach declares certain kinds of human behavior to be wrong without discerning all the circumstantial differences.

General Bibliography

Albert, Ethel M., Theodore C. Denise, and Sheldon P. Peterfreund, eds. *Great Traditions in Ethics.* 6th ed. Belmont, Calif.: Wadsworth, 1988.

Arendt, Hannah. *The Human Condition.* Garden City, N.Y.: Doubleday, Anchor Books, 1959.

Aristotle. *A New Aristotle Reader.* Edited by J. L. Ackrill. Princeton: N.J.: Princeton University Press, 1987.

Ashmore, Robert B. *Building a Moral System.* Englewood Cliffs, N.J.: Prentice-Hall, 1987.

Battaglia, Anthony. *Toward a Reformulation of Natural Law.* New York: Seabury Press, 1981.

Baum, Robert J. *Ethics and Engineering Curricula.* Hastings, N.Y.: The Hastings Center, 1980.

Beauchamp, Tom L. *Philosophical Ethics: An Introduction to Moral Philosophy.* New York: McGraw-Hill, 1982.

Beauchamp, Tom L., and Norman E. Bowie. *Ethical Theory and Business.* Englewood Cliffs, N.J.: Prentice-Hall, 1983.

Bell, Derrick. *And We Are Not Saved: The Elusive Quest for Racial Justice.* New York: Basic Books, 1987.

Bellah, Robert N., et al. *Habits of the Heart: Individualism and Commitment in American Life.* New York: Perennial Library, Harper & Row, 1985.

Berdyaev, Nicolas. *The Destiny of Man.* New York: Harper & Row, 1960.

Bok, Sissela. *Lying: Moral Choice in Public and Private Life.* New York: Pantheon Books, 1978.

Bourke, Vernon J. *History of Ethics: A Comprehensive Survey of the History of Ideas from the Early Greeks to the Present Time.* New York: Doubleday, 1968.

Buber, Martin. *I and Thou.* Translated by Walter Kaufmann. New York: Charles Scribner's Sons, 1970.

Calderone, Mary S., ed. *Sexuality and Human Values.* New York: Association Press, 1974.

Callahan, Daniel, and Sissela Bok, eds. *Ethics Teaching in Higher Education.* New York: Plenum Press, 1980.

Christians, Clifford G. *Teaching Ethics in Journalism Education.* Hastings, N.Y.: The Hastings Center, 1980.

Clouser, K. Danner. *Teaching Bioethics: Strategies, Problems, and Resources.* Hastings, N.Y.: The Hastings Center, 1980.

Cousins, Norman. *Anatomy of an Illness as Perceived by the Patient.* New York: W. W. Norton, 1979.

Curran, Charles E. *Issues in Sexual and Medical Ethics.* Notre Dame: University of Notre Dame Press, 1978.

Davis, Angela Y. *Women, Race & Class.* New York: Vintage Books, 1983.

De George, Richard T. *Business Ethics.* New York: Macmillan, 1982.

Demetrakopoulos, Stephanie. *Listening to Our Bodies: The Rebirth of Feminine Wisdom.* Boston, Beacon Press, 1983.

Dewey, John, and James H. Tufts. *Ethics.* Rev. ed. New York: Henry Holt, 1932.

Donagan, Alan. *The Theory of Morality.* Chicago: University of Chicago Press, 1977.

Douglas, Mary. *Purity and Danger: An Analysis of Concepts of Pollution and Taboo.* London: Routledge & Kegan Paul, 1966.

Edel, May, and Abraham Edel. *Anthropology and Ethics.* Springfield, Ill.: Charles C. Thomas, 1959.

Elkins, Stanley M. *Slavery.* New York: Universal Library, Grosset & Dunlap, 1963.

Fleishman, Joel L., and Bruce L. Payne. *Ethical Dilemmas and the Education of Policymakers.* Hastings, N.Y.: The Hastings Center, 1980.

Fletcher, Joseph. *Situation Ethics.* Philadelphia: Westminster Press, 1966.

Frankena, William K., and John T. Granrose, eds. *Introductory Readings in Ethics.* Englewood Cliffs, N.J.: Prentice-Hall, 1974.

Gaylin, Willard. *Feelings: Our Vital Signs.* New York: Harper & Row, 1979.

Gilligan, Carol. *In a Different Voice.* Cambridge, Mass.: Harvard University Press, 1982.

Girvetz, Harry K. *Beyond Right and Wrong.* New York: Free Press, 1973.

Gray, J. Glenn. *The Warriors: Reflections on Men in Battle.* New York: Harper Torchbooks, 1967.

Harrison, Beverly Wildung. *Making the Connections: Essays in Feminist Social Ethics.* Boston: Beacon Press, 1985.

Heilbroner, Robert L. *An Inquiry into the Human Prospect.* New York: W. W. Norton, 1975.

Heyd, David. *Supererogation: Its Status in Ethical Theory.* New York: Cambridge University Press, 1982.

Hoehn, Richard A. *Up from Apathy: A Study of Moral Awareness and Social Involvement.* Nashville: Abingdon Press, 1983.

Hollenbach, David. *Claims in Conflict.* New York: Paulist Press, 1979.

Johnson, James Turner. *Just War Tradition and the Restraint of War.* Princeton, N.J.: Princeton University Press, 1981.

Joubert, Laurent. *Treatise on Laughter.* Translated by Gregory deRocher. Birmingham: University of Alabama Press, 1980.

Kagan, Jerome, and Sharon Lamb. *The Emergence of Morality in Young Children.* Chicago: University of Chicago Press, 1987.

Kammer, Charles L., III. *Ethics and Liberation.* Maryknoll, N.Y.: Orbis Books, 1988.

Kelly, Michael J. *Legal Ethics and Legal Education.* Hastings, N.Y.: The Hastings Center, 1980.

Kennedy, Eugene C. *The New Sexuality: Myth, Fables and Hang-Ups.* New York: Doubleday, 1973.

King, Martin Luther, Jr. *Why We Can't Wait.* New York: American Library, 1964.

Kluger, Richard. *Simple Justice: The History of "Brown v. Board of Education" and Black America's Struggle for Equality*. New York: Vintage Books, 1977.

Kolbenschlag, Madonna. *Kiss Sleeping Beauty Good-Bye: Breaking the Spell of Feminine Myths and Models*. Garden City, N.Y.: Doubleday, 1979.

Kosnik, Anthony, et al. *Human Sexuality*. New York: Paulist Press, 1977.

Kubler-Ross, Elisabeth. *On Death and Dying*. New York: Macmillan, 1972.

Kurtz, Lester R. *The Nuclear Cage: A Sociology of the Arms Race*. Englewood Cliffs, N.J.: Prentice-Hall, 1988.

Lammers, Stephen E., and Allen Verhey. *On Moral Medicine*. Grand Rapids, Mich.: William B. Eerdmans, 1987.

Lepp, Ignace. *The Authentic Morality*. New York: Macmillan, 1970.

Lewis, Anthony. *Gideon's Trumpet*. New York: Vintage Books, 1966.

Lonergan, Bernard. *Insight: A Study of Human Understanding*. New York: Longmans, Philosophical Library, 1957.

Lorenz, Konrad. *On Aggression*. New York: Harcourt Brace Jovanovich, 1966.

McCormick, Richard. *How Brave a New World: Dilemmas in Bioethics*. Garden City, N.Y.: Doubleday, 1981.

Macintyre, Alasdair. *After Virtue*. Notre Dame: University of Notre Dame Press, 1982.

Macklin, Ruth. *Mortal Choices: Ethical Dilemmas in Modern Medicine*. Boston: Houghton Mifflin, 1987.

Macmurray, John. *Reason and Emotion*. London: Faber & Faber, 1935.

Maguire, Daniel C. *The Moral Choice*. Garden City, N.Y.: Doubleday, 1978, New York: Harper & Row, 1979.

———. *A New American Justice*. New York: Harper & Row, 1980.

———. *Death By Choice*. Garden City, N.Y., Image Books, 1984.

———. *The Moral Revolution*. New York: Harper & Row, 1986.

Mahatma Gandhi. *Gandhi on Non-Violence*. Edited by Thomas Merton. New York: New Directions, 1965.

Midgley, Mary, *Animals and Why They Matter*. Athens, Ga.: University of Georgia Press, 1983.

Montagu, Ashley. *On Being Human*. New York: Hawthorn Books, 1966.

Morreall, John. *Taking Laughter Seriously*. Albany: State University of New York Press, 1983.

———, ed. *The Philosophy of Laughter and Humor*. Albany: State University of New York Press, 1987.

Munsey, Brenda, ed. *Moral Development, Moral Education and Kohlberg*. Birmingham: Religious Education Press, 1980.

Nelson, James B. *Embodiment*. Minneapolis: Augsburg, 1978.

Nietzsche, Friedrich. *Genealogy of Morals: Collected Works*. New York: Russell & Russell, 1964.

Nisbet, Robert. *The Sociological Tradition*. New York: Basic Books, 1966.

Noddings, Nel. *Women and Evil*. Berkeley, Calif.: University of California Press, 1989.

———. *Caring: A Feminine Approach to Ethics & Moral Education*. Berkeley, Calif.: University of California Press, 1984.

Nolan, Richard T., and Frank G. Kirkpatrick. *Living Issues in Ethics*. Belmont, Calif.: Wadsworth, 1982.

Perelman, Chaim H. *Justice*. New York: Random House, 1967.

Piaget, Jean. *The Moral Judgment of the Child*. New York: Harcourt-Brace, 1932.

————. *Six Psychological Studies*. New York: Vintage Books, 1968.

Pieper, Josef. *Leisure: The Basis of Culture*. New York: Mentor-Omega, 1963.

Plato. *Laws, Gorgias, Republic, Symposium*.

Powers, Charles W., and David Vogel. *Ethics in the Education of Business Managers*. Hastings, N.Y.: The Hastings Center, 1980.

Porter, Burton F. *The Good Life: Alternatives in Ethics*. New York: Macmillan, 1980.

Rachels, James, ed. *Moral Problems: A Collection of Philosophical Essays*. 3rd ed. New York: Harper & Row, 1979.

Rand, Ayn. *The Virtue of Selfishness*. New York: New American Library, Signet Books, 1964.

Rosen, Bernard, and Arthur L. Caplan. *Ethics in the Undergraduate Curriculum*. Hastings, N.Y.: The Hastings Center, 1980.

Sabini, John, and Maury Silver. *Moralities of Everyday Life*. Oxford: Oxford University Press, 1982.

Sapp, Gary L., ed. *Handbook of Moral Development*. Birmingham: Religious Education Press, 1986.

Sartre, Jean-Paul. *L'Existentialisme est un humanisme*. Paris: Editions Nagel, 1959.

Scheler, Max. *Formalism in Ethics and Non-Formal Ethics of Values*. Translated by Manfred S. Frings and Roger L. Funk. 5th rev. ed. Evanston, Ill.: Northwestern University Press, 1973.

Schell, Jonathan. *The Fate of the Earth*. New York: Alfred A. Knopf, 1982.

Schopenhauer, Arthur. *The Basis of Morality*. 2nd. ed. London: George Allen & Unwin, 1915.

Shannon, Thomas A., ed. *Bioethics*. 3d ed. Mahwah, N.J.: Paulist Press, 1987.

Sharp, Gene. *The Politics of Nonviolent Action*. 3 vols. Boston: Porter Sargent, 1973.

Sivard, Ruth Leger. *World Military and Social Expenditures*. Washington: World Priorities, published annually.

Smith, Adam. *The Theory of Moral Sentiments*. New York: Augustus M. Kelley, 1966.

Solomon, Robert C. *Ethics: A Brief Introduction*. New York: McGraw-Hill, 1984.

————. *Morality and the Good Life: An Introduction to Ethics through Classical Sources*. New York: McGraw-Hill, 1984.

Solovyev, Vladimir. *The Meaning of Love*. London: Geoffrey Bles, Centenary Press, 1945.

Spinoza, Baruch. *Ethics*. New York: Dover Publications, 1951.

State of the World: A Worldwatch Institute Report on Progress toward a Sustainable Society. New York: W. W. Norton, 1989.

Thomas Aquinas. *Summa Theologica*.

Tribe, Laurence H. *Abortion: The Clash of Absolutes*. Boston: W. W. Norton, 1990.

Vivas, Eliseo. *The Moral Life and the Ethical Life*. Chicago: University of Chicago Press, 1950.

Walzer, Michael. *Just and Unjust Wars: A Moral Argument with Historical Illustration*. New York: Basic Books, 1977.

——. *Spheres of Justice*. New York: Basic Books, 1983.

Warwick, Donald P. *The Teaching of Ethics in the Social Sciences*. Hastings, N.Y.: The Hastings Center, 1980.

Wasserstrom, Richard A., ed. *Morality and the Law*. Belmont, Calif.: Wadsworth, 1971.

Index